SECRETS OF SUCCESSFUL SEX MANIACS

* Love thy neighbor all through the day. But first make sure her husband's away.

* If you're not as good as you once were, then at least be as good as you ever were.

* Have no aversions to mergins with virgins, though it's more fun to pet with a well-seasoned vet.

* Always bare her in mind.

* Carry a new instrument of credit created specially for bawdyhouses: Bangamericard!

THE OFFICIAL SEX MANIACS JOKE BOOK

by Larry Wilde

Illustrations by Ron Wing

PINNACLE BOOKS • NEW YORK CITY

CONTENTS

SEX MANIAC

A guy who goes to the zoo, sees an elephant and screams, "Wow! What a perfect 436-226-336!"

THE LOVERS

Phil stood at the perfume counter listening to the salesgirl. "Here's one called 'Perhaps' that sells for thirty-five dollars an ounce," she said.

"Thirty-five dollars an ounce!" exclaimed the young Don Juan. "For thirty-five bucks I don't want 'Perhaps,' I want 'For Sure'!"

* * *

When Danny was in the hospital, he had a day nurse and a night nurse. In the afternoon he rested.

* * *

"But, Robert," she gasped, "why did you park here when there are so many nicer spots farther down the road?"

He stopped what he was doing just long enough to mutter, "Because I believe in love at first site."

1

TESSIE'S TESTIMONIAL
Ted isn't as good as he once was, but he's as good once as he ever was.

* * *

"Hello, is this the Salvation Army?"
"Yes, it is."
"Do you save bad girls?"
"Yes, we do."
"How about saving me one for Saturday night?"

* * * *

Stopping at the first house on his famous ride, Paul Revere cried, "Is your husband home?"

"Yes!" replied the woman.

"Then tell him to get dressed so he can fight the British!"

At the second, third, and fourth houses he asked the same question, got the same answer, and left the same instructions.

At the fifth house, he again shouted, "Is your husband home?"

"No!" came the reply. "He'll be gone a week."

"Whoa-a-a!"

* * *

SNOW JOB
What a lover uses on a woman to defrost her

"I know a girl who's a nymphomaniac, but she had to give it up!"
"Why?"
"It took up too much of her time!"

*   *   *

A pretty airline stewardess walked into a bar wearing a pair of tight-fitting slacks. You could see every ripple of her flesh as she sashayed up to a stool and sat down.

A fellow, right beside her, said, "Hey, honey, how do you get into those pants?"

"Well," said the hostess, "you can start by buying me a martini!"

*   *   *

She: Aren't the stars pretty tonight?
He: Can't tell. I'm in no position to say.

*   *   *

PICKUP
A date that a man is so embarrassed to be seen with, he gets her into bed and climbs on top to hide her

*   *   *

Breathes there a man with a soul so dead,
Who's never to his girlfriend said,
"To hell with breakfast,
Come back to bed!"

A little brown dog was running across a freight yard, crossing all the railroad tracks, until a switch engine nipped off the end of his tail. The canine yelped, spun around, and when he tried to bite the train, he got his head chopped off.

MORAL: *Never lose your head over a piece of tail.*

* * *

After a wild night together, lover boy looked down and asked, "Do you tell your mother everything you do?"

"Certainly not!" she retorted. "My mother couldn't care less. It's my husband who's so damn inquisitive!"

* * *

RED SONG
She Was Only a Communist's Daughter but Everybody Got His Share.

* * *

If there were only three women in the world, what would they be doing?

Two of them would be off in a corner somewhere talking about the third.

But what if there were only three men in the world, what would they be doing?

Running themselves ragged trying to find three women.

4

He: If I were to steal a kiss, what would
   you say?
She: You're as dumb as the guy who had
   a chance at a Cadillac and took only the
   windshield wiper.

*   *   *

After a recent Broadway revival of
Hamlet, the newspaper critic chatted with
the leading man. "Is it your opinion,"
asked the reporter, "that Shakespeare in-
tended us to understand that Hamlet had
sexual relations with Ophelia?"

"I don't know what Shakespeare in-
tended," replied the actor, "but I always
do!"

*   *   *

An actor had just passed a night of
pleasure with a girl he met in his hotel
lobby. As he dressed in the morning, he
paused for a moment to give the girl a
little envelope.

"Here are two tickets to my show" he
said.

The girl looked up in amazement. "I
don't want your tickets. I'm hungry. I
want bread."

"If you want bread," he said, "sleep
with a baker. I'm an actor. Here're two
tickets to my show."

OVERHEARD AT A COCKTAIL PARTY

Smooth dude: Would you like to have breakfast with me tomorrow morning?

Flaky fox: Sounds good!

Smooth dude: Shall I phone you or nudge you?

*   *   *

I have no aversions
To mergin's with virgins,
Though it's more fun to pet
With a well-seasoned vet.

*   *   *

SAVOIR-FAIRE

When you're loving a man's wife, and he breaks down the door, stands there and says, "Go ahead!" and you can go ahead.

*   *   *

Jake and Morris, two Las Vegas habitués, were standing at the Rivera bar eyeing the ladies when the cute redheaded cigarette girl passed. "Gee," said Jake, "I feel like having that redhead again!"

"Huh?" said Morris, "You mean you've *had* that doll?"

"No, but I *felt* like it last night, too!"

6

Benny Wildman, New Jersey's fashion forerunner in men's wear, tells about the lover who walked up to the haberdashery counter of a large department store.

He was greeted by a shapely clerk. "Good afternoon," she murmured, "and what is your desire?"

"My desire," he said, after looking her over appreciatively, "is to sweep you into my arms, rush you out of this store and up to my apartment, mix a pitcher of martinis, put on some soft music, and make mad, passionate love to you. But what I *need* is a pair of socks."

* * *

"He kissed me a number of times before we quarreled, but then we finally made up."

"Then I suppose he kissed you all over again."

"No, mostly on the lips."

* * *

A Frenchman and an American were discussing love in America. "In France," said the Frenchman, "we have variety. There are 118 ways of making love."

"118?" said the American, "I know of only four. There's the normal way . . ."

"Ah," interrupted the Frenchman, "119!"

Charlie met Gloria at a cocktail lounge. After a few drinks he said, "Let's go back to my pad. My dog Rex can make drinks, and he does great tricks with girls!"

"Hold it!" snapped Gloria. "I don't go that route!"

Three martinis later, Gloria relented and they went to Charlie's apartment. His dog Rex fixed them vodka gimlets. "My," said Gloria, "ain't he clever." In twenty minutes, Rex prepared two more.

Feeling pretty good now, Gloria asked, "What about those tricks your dog does with chicks?"

"Just pop in the bedroom with Rex," said Charlie, "and take off your clothes."

In they went. After ten minutes had passed, Charlie followed. The girl was lying naked on the bed, and the dog was on the dresser peering out the window. "You said your dog did great tricks with girls in bed," exclaimed Gloria. "He hasn't done a thing!"

"Damn it, Rex!" said Charlie, removing his jacket and then unbuttoning his shirt. "I'm going to show you this trick only one more time!"

Rex, I'm going to show you this trick only one more time!

9

THREE STAGES OF MAN'S LIFE
1. *Tri-weekly*
2. *Try weekly*
3. *Try weakly*

* * *

LOVE NEST
Where a girl who offers no resistance
leads a very nice existence

* * *

Hobnobbing at the bar one night, Finnegan and Duffy bragged about their conquests. "I met a gal once," claimed Finnegan, "and within one hour we was home in bed."

"One time when I was fishing, I saw three girls swimming naked," bragged Duffy. "I took the first one behind a bush, and after we were finished she jumped up and turned a somersault in the air. 'What's that for?' I asked. 'So I won't get pregnant!' she replied.

"Well, from then on, I had one on the ground and two in the air the rest of the afternoon."

* * * *

She: So you think of me whenever you're away, darling?
He: Yes, honey, I always bare you in mind.

Wyoming track star Tony Poulos says a successful romance is a matter of perfect timing: The girl has to give in just before the guy gives up.

* * *

A well-stacked young blonde strolled up to the floor manager in a large department store. "Pardon me," she said, "do you have notions on this floor?"

"Yes, miss," he replied, taking in all her physical assets, "but we have to suppress them during business hours."

* * *

POST OFFICE POP
She's Only a Mailman's Daughter but She Sure Delivers the Goods.

* * *

Natalie: My, what long, slim, expressive hands you have! They belong on a girl.
Nick: You win, honey!

* * *

He was making mad love to the girl he just met when suddenly he cried, "Quick, kiss me! Kiss me!"

"Kiss you?" she said, "I shouldn't even be doing this!"

11

Randolph walked into his health club trying to hide his "shiner." "Where'd you get that black eye?" asked one of the members.

"From a cough."

"From a cough?"

"Yeah," replied Randolph, "I coughed in a clothes closet."

* * *

Dress manufacturer:..What salary do you expect?

Model: Two hundred dollars a week.

Dress manufacturer: I'll pay you that with pleasure.

Model: Oh, no you won't! With pleasure it'll cost you $250 a week.

* * *

TRUE LOVE

An injection with affection
to the midsection from a projection,
without objection

* * *

He begged and pleaded for more,
But she said, "We've already done four!
   And I'm sure you've heard,
   Even though it's absurd,
That Eros spelled backwards is *sore*."

She gave him a long, lingering, wet kiss, waved goodnight, and shut her apartment door. But he was aroused to such fervor, he broke down the door, grabbed the girl, threw her to the floor, and began pumping away.

In seven minutes, it was all over. "You really enjoyed that, didn't you?" he said. "I could tell 'cause your toes are all curled up!"

"Of course they're curled!" said the girl. "I've still got my panty hose on!"

* * *

It was three o'clock in the morning. The angry father yelled down to his daughter in the living room. "Evelyn, is that boy there yet?"

"Not quite," she whispered hoarsely, "but he's getting there!"

* * *

In the game of *love* we claim
There's only one reward.
It isn't how you played the game
But how many times you've scored.

* * *

THE THREE BEST THINGS IN
LIFE
A martini before and a nap after

13

EXPENSE ACCOUNT FOR JULY AND AUGUST

7/1	Ad for female secretary	$3.50
7/2	Violets for new secretary	2.00
7/8	Week's salary for new secretary	100.00
7/9	Roses for secretary	15.00
7/11	Candy for wife	1.25
7/13	Lunch with secretary	9.00
7/15	Week's salary for secretary	125.00
7/16	Movie tickets (self and wife)	2.50
7/18	Theater tickets (self and secretary)	20.00
7/19	Ice cream soda for wife	.50
7/22	Virginia's salary	150.00
7/23	Champagne and dinner for Ginny	8.60
8/29	Doctor	500.00
8/30	Fur coat for wife	3,200.00
8/31	Ad for male secretary	3.50
		$4,180.85

* * *

"Where are you?"
"I'm hiding!"
"Where are you?"
"I'm hiding."
"Where are you? I want to seduce you!"
"I'm hiding in the closet!"

14

Rocky hadn't been too lucky with the ladies lately and so he stared incredulously from his upper berth at a blonde getting undressed in a lower berth on the Chicago Limited.

The woman slowly took off her wig, then removed a glass eye and her falsies. As she reached down to unscrew her wooden leg she spotted Rocky peeping at her. "All right. What do you want?" she asked.

"You know what I want!" slobbered Rocky. "Unscrew it and throw it up here!"

*　　*　　*

Comedy star Marty Ingels includes this favorite for friends:

The ladies of the harem were seated in a circle, casting dice on a gorgeous Persian rug. Around the circle went the cubes in the hands of the excited players.

"It's Zenobia tonight!" they screamed in unison. "Poor Zenobia!"

With a deep sigh Zenobia arose and with dragging steps passed through the velvet portieres.

"I'd hate to be that poor kid," remarked Little Persia "That's the third time this week she's had to wash the dishes!"

*　　*　　*

When the Sultan entered his harem unexpectedly, his wives let out a terrified sheik.

The Sultan called for his eunuch. "I am in the mood," he said. "Bring me wife number 256."

So the eunuch ran out of the palace and into the harem. He ran through the garden, past the orchard, and up the steps. And he soon returned with wife 256.

A little later, the Sultan sent for his eunuch again. "I want more! Go get wife number 87."

And the eunuch ran through the palace, to the harem, through the garden, the orchard, and then up the steps. He brought back wife 87.

Then the Sultan asked for wife 49. Again the eunuch raced to the harem. When he returned with number 49 he was panting heavily. Then he suddenly collapsed and died.

MORAL: *It's not the women in your life that can kill you—it's the chasing after them.*

16

It's not the women in your life that can kill you—it's the chasing after them!

17

A Sultan whose loves grew so vastly,
Just couldn't love any steadfastly.
  Someone asked him in fun
  If he'd slept twice with one.
He replied, "Such a thought is most
  ghastly."

* * *

Russell had worked and traveled all over the world. "For a while I held the post of chief spitter in the Sultan's harem," he told a friend.

"What in the world is a chief spitter?"

"All I had to do," explained Russell, "was to spit on each of the Sultan's wives; when one sizzled, I would take her to the Sultan.

* * *

The Sultan had nine wives. Eight of them had it pretty soft.

* * *

While vacationing in the north woods, Eddie thought it might be nice to write his girl. He walked into town and entered the only general store. There behind the counter stood a voluptuous young blonde. "Do you keep stationery?" asked Eddie.

"Well," she replied, "I do until the last few seconds, and then I just go crazy!"

A farmhand was testifying as to the character of a woman defendant. The prosecutor asked, "What about her veracity?"

"Wa-a-al," said the farmer, "some sez she does and some sez she doesn't!"

*   *   *

A ventriloquist at a summer camp was amazing the neighboring farmhands with his talents. He threw his voice so it sounded like a horse standing nearby said, "Hello there, Zeke!"

Then he made the cow moo: "Oh, my aching teats!"

He was looking thoughtfully at a flock of sheep nearby when one of the hired hands shouted, "Listen, if that little ewe at the end says anything, she's a goddam liar."

*   *   *

Claude complained to another farmhand, Reuben, that he couldn't get to sleep at night.

"Whyncha try countin' sheep?" suggested Reuben.

That night in bed, Claude decided to take his friend's advice and began counting: "One, two, three, hello, sweetheart, five, six ..."

A traveling salesman staying overnight at a farmhouse was proudly being shown around the place by the farmer. "Built this place with my own hands," he boasted, "and I made everything the hard way. See that floor? Didn't use no nails— the whole thing is dovetailed. The hard way.

"See that ceiling? Didn't use no joists —the whole thing is hanging from a flying beam. The hard way!"

Just then the farmer's pretty daughter entered the room. The salesman looked at him quizzically.

"Yup," said the farmer, "standing up in a canoe."

* * *

Tom Stout, TWA's popular good will ambassador, regales waiting passengers at LAX with stories like this:

A traveling salesman's car broke down, and he was given a room for the night by an attractive woman living alone. He couldn't sleep. Suddenly he heard a light rapping at the door. "Would you like some company?" she asked, appearing at the door in her dressing gown.

"You bet I would!" said the salesman anxiously.

"Good!" declared the woman, " 'Cause here's another fella whose car broke down and he needs a room for the night!"

"Well," said the farmer to the traveling salesman, "we don't get many visitors this far off the beaten track, but since your car broke down, you'll have to sleep either with the baby or in the barn."

"I'll take the barn," said the traveling man, envisioning the baby wetting him in his slumber.

The next morning, a beautiful young girl walked into the barn to milk the cow. "Who are you?" asked the salesman.

"I'm the baby of the family," she replied. "Who are you?"

"I'm the jackass who slept in the barn!"

*　　*　　*

A traveling salesman took a girl up to his hotel room. He poured her a glass of whiskey and as he added the soda, he looked up and said, "Say when!"

"Can't I even have my drink first?"

*　　*　　*

TRAVELING MAN'S TOAST

Here's to the girl with the turned-up nose,
The turned-in eyes, and the turned-down toes,
With the turned-on heart and the turned-down light—
The hunch I had turned out all right.

A salesman met a gal at one of those singles' bars on Friday night. "Look," he said to her, "I'm only in town for a couple of hours, and I can't waste time. Do you fool around or don't you?"

"Well," said the girl shyly, "I don't usually, but you talked me into it!"

*　　*　　*

"Doc, I just can't help it. The only thing on my mind these days is sex."

"My advice to you is just stop thinking about it. Scientists have just discovered that people who think too much about sex often lose their hearing."

"Is that a fact?"

"What did you say?"

*　　*　　*

"Young woman," said the doctor, "I'd like to give you a thorough examination."

"But," said the cute co-ed, "Dr. Jones found me perfect last week."

"So he told me," said the M.D.

*　　*　　*

The girl from Tennessee was in the hospital for a check-up. "Have you ever been X-rayed?" asked the doctor.

"Nope," she said, "but ah've been ultra-violated!"

I'll kiss it—that'll make it better!

23

"Is Dr. Moore egotistical?"

"I'll say. He's so conceited that when he takes a woman's pulse, he subtracts ten beats for his personality."

* * *

Max was 85. "You gotta help me, doctor," he pleaded. "I got a date with a 23-year-old secretary and I want to be sure that I'm able to perform. Can you give me something to pep me up?"

The physician smiled, wrote out a prescription, and had the old duck fill it. Later that night, out of curiosity, he telephoned him.

"Did the medicine help any?" asked the M.D.

"It was great!" replied the old man. "I've managed three times already!"

"Swell," said the doctor. "What about the girl?"

"Oh, she hasn't gotten here yet!"

* * *

Two gentlemen, both octogenarians, were sitting in their club discussing sex. "Tell me," said the 82-year-old, "how often do you try it?"

"Once a month, every month," answered the 86-year-old. "Except in July and August."

"Why not then?"

"'Cause that's when the man who puts me on and off goes on vacation!"

MacGregor, aged 78, went into a drugstore to purchase some contraceptives. The woman clerk rang up the sale on the cash register and said, "That'll be 1.59 with tax."

"Never mind the tax," said MacGregor. "I'll tie them on with a string!"

* * *

Grandpappy Dawson, close onto 90, walked into a drugstore and said to the clerk, "I'd like to get ten cents worth of that stuff they put in the soldier's food so they won't have any amorous desires."

"Why, Gramps," snickered the druggist, "you wouldn't be having any need for that."

"Maybe not, but I thought if I could take a pinch through my nose I could get it off my mind."

* * *

The family was pretty disturbed when the eldest of the clan, Grandpa David, aged 79, announced that he was getting married. They were particularly horrified to learn that the new bride was only 22 years old.

"Look, Pop," said his oldest son. "You— marrying a young girl like that—it could be fatal!"

"So what?" said the old man. "If she dies, I'll marry again!"

Mr. Stein, who was pushing 80, was advised by his doctor that he needed "mother's milk." When Stein informed his wife, she suggested that he see Mrs. Finkel, their neighbor, who had just given birth and had plenty to spare.

Stein went next door and explained his predicament. The woman felt sorry for the old man and said she'd be happy to oblige.

Mrs. Finkel stripped to the waist and Stein went to work. After ten minutes of this, the woman became a little excited. "Is there anything else you'd like, maybe?" asked the milk donor.

"Well," said Stein, "maybe you could get me a couple of cookies?"

Greenberg, aged 75, had been selling newspapers on the same street corner for over thirty years. And suddenly he was gone. Disappeared. Three weeks went by and just when his customers feared the worst, Greenberg was back on his corner doing business as usual.

"Where've you been?" asked a steady customer.

"One day, three weeks ago," explained the old man, "a gorgeous blonde walked up to me with a policeman and accused me of being the father of her child. I was so proud—I pleaded guilty."

*   *   *

Diana was the talk of all her friends— most of it behind her back. "We just don't understand," said one of her friends. "Why does a young girl like you carry on with a 90-year-old man?"

"Listen, dearie," she explained, "if someone handed you a check for a million dollars, would you stop to examine the date?"

*   *   *

LOVE FOR SALE

When you knock at her door and her husband opens it—sell something, brother! Sell something!

One good thing about sex—it brings lovers so close together they can't see anything wrong with each other.

* * *

Sam was sitting at a bar beside a striking brunette, fascinated by her capacity for Manhattans. She kept ordering them one after another. As she gulped down her fourth in rapid succession, Sam leaned over and said, "Would five make you dizzy?"

"The price is all right," she replied, "but the name is Daisy!"

* * *

What happens when a girl named Perfect meets a man named Practice?

* * *

"I met a chick that's really naive," said Felix to his buddy. "When I asked her if she knew the difference between a Caesar salad and sexual intercourse, she said she had no idea."

"Did you explain it to her?" asked his friend.

"Hell, no!" said Felix. "But I have lunch with her every day."

Betty Lou allowed herself to be picked up at a bar and after a few drinks went to the guy's apartment. While he was changing into "something more comfortable," Betty Lou was intrigued by a large brass button marked PUSH.

She pushed, a secret panel slid up and she stepped into a completely outfitted torture chamber, with whips, Iron Maidens, branding irons, and an operating table with a bucketful of damp sponges below.

Betty Lou felt a catch in her throat when she noticed the windows were barred and the door bolted. Frightened, she tried another room, the den this time. Animal heads decorated the walls here. She began to tremble.

Suddenly her host entered behind her wearing a yellow silk dressing gown, his eyes slit evilly.

"W-w-what are you going to do to me?" she asked trembling.

While she cowered in fear he looked at her intently and said, "I'm going to rape you!"

"Oh, thank God!" she sighed audibly.

* * *

JUDICIAL JUDGMENT
Rape is impossible. A woman can run faster with her dress up than a man with his pants down.

The entire courtroom sat in stony silence as the accused man offered his explanation: "Your honor, I wasn't within a mile of where this dame says the assault took place. Besides that, it wasn't an assault because she asked me to do it. And besides that, this ain't the dame I raped."

* * *

A man was accused of raping a woman leaning over the railing of her front porch. The judge questioned the woman. "What did you do when he started pushing you?"

"I pushed right back," said the woman. "Nobody's gonna push me off my own front porch!"

* * *

The mountaineer was about to be sentenced for statutory rape. He objected that the girl consented and she was over sixteen anyhow. "The law has been changed," said the judge. "The legal age of consent is now eighteen."

"Then before you sentence me, your honor, can I have a week out on bail?" asked the man. "I want to tell a couple of friends of mine that they're working under the old ruling!"

31

The accused was a little man, no more than five feet tall. His accuser was an amazon of a woman, over six feet tall. Yet here they were in court. The man was charged with rape. The magistrate, who was a pretty good judge of distance, pondered for a moment and then spoke to the woman: "It isn't that I don't believe you, madam, but you're so tall and he's so short. It seems almost impossible that your charge could be true."

"Your honor, it is true!" shouted the woman. "Although I admit I did stoop a little!"

33

RAPE
1. *Assault with intent to please*
2. *Seduction without salesmanship*

* * *

I met a woman who was willin'.
Now I'm takin' penicillin.

* * *

A girl rushed into a lawyer's office. "I want him arrested! He threw me on the bed. He ... Oh, it was awful!"

"Now calm down," soothed the attorney. "Let's get the whole story straight. What did he do first?"

"He locked the door!"

"Aha, kidnapping!" said the lawyer, writing on a pad. "Ten years. Then what did he do?"

"He pulled up my dress."

"Indecent exposure. Two more years." He made a note. "Then what?"

"He put his hand on my ... my ..."

"It's all right, I understand. Attempted assault. Five years. And then what?"

"He threw me on the bed."

"Ah, hah! Mayhem and felonious constraint. Ten to fifteen years. And then?"

"Then ... he did it to me!"

"That does it! Rape! Twenty years— maybe we can get him the chair. And meanwhile you were screaming and struggling ..."

"Well-l-l, not exactly. It was kind of late, and I didn't want to disturb everybody, and . . ."

"Oh, for God's sake!" cried the lawyer, tearing up his notes, "that's just a plain ordinary screw!"

* * *

SALESMANSHIP
Ability to turn rape into rapture

* * *

A fellow in the park was doing push-ups. A drunk staggered up to him and said, "What's the matta, fella, did you lose your girl?"

* * *

"That man made love to me, Judge," said the plaintiff in the breach of promise suit. "He promised to marry me, and then he married another woman. He broke my heart and I want $10,000!"

She got it.

The next case was a damage suit brought by a woman who had been run over by an automobile and had three ribs broken. She was awarded $275.

MORAL: *Don't break their hearts, men. Kick 'em in the ribs!*

LOVERS LAMENT

The frustration the first time you can't make it the second time is nothing compared to the second time you can't make it the first time.

* * *

Two Michigan State football stars, Tom and Greg, took two pretty co-eds out for a ride in their car. They drove twenty miles out from the campus and parked on a lonely stretch of road. "Now we're gonna proceed with this *hereafter date*," announced Tom.

"What's a *hereafter date*?" asked one of the girls.

"If you aren't here after what we're here after, you're gonna be here after we're gone."

* * *

It was their first date and they were both thinking of the same thing. She called it mental telepathy; he called it beginner's luck.

* * *

A beautiful moon shone down on the parked car in which sat Gayle and her bashful boyfriend Rick.

"Dear," murmured Gayle, "you remind me of Don Juan, the great lover!"

"Really?" replied Rick. "Why?"

"For one thing," said Gayle, "he's been dead for years!"

* * *

Walter Painter, the superbly gifted Hollywood choreographer, eavesdropped on Dominic, Mickey, and Gabe who were having a brew after their bowling match. The subject got around to women. "Gimme a girl of 20," said Dominic. "They're old enough to know how, but young enough to learn new tricks!"

"Ah!" said Mickey. "I like 'em around 30. By that age they're just beginning to mellow."

"Give me a girl of 40!" announced Gabe.

"Forty?" asked his cronies unbelievingly.

"That's the best age for a woman. They don't yell, they don't tell, they don't swell, and they appreciate it like hell!"

* * *

DITTY
I Can't Get Over a Girl Like You So Get Up and Answer the Phone Yourself.

It took thousands of years for man to learn to walk on his hind legs, but even today his eyes still swing from limb to limb.

* * *

A LOVER'S LOOK AT THE FEMALE

From 15 to 20, women are like Africa—
   Part virgin and part explored.

From 21 to 35, women are like Asia—
   Hot and exotic.

From 35, to 45, they are like the United States—
   Fully explored and free with their resources.

From 45 to 55, they are like Europe—
   Exhausted, but still interesting in places.

From 55 on, they are like Australia—
   Everybody knows it's down there but nobody cares very much.

* * *

Roger took Elaine for a ride in his new car. They drove out to Lover's Lane. Just before they got there the car stalled. Roger and Elaine got out to push. Roger pushed and Elaine pushed and while they were pushing, somebody stole the car.

Wright King, the talented stage and screen actor, passed this one along:

Marty had his arms around a shapely blonde. "Baby," he breathed, "you're the whole world to me. I can't live without you. I love . . ."

At that moment the doorbell rang. The blonde jumped up. "It's my husband!" she gasped. "You've got to go. Hurry, please!"

"But where am I gonna go?" asked Marty. "I can't go out the door. Your husband'll see me!"

"Then quick, jump out the window!"

"But we're on the 13th floor!"

"So what?" she rasped. "This is no time to be superstitious!"

* * *

Poor Shirley, between dishes and douches she's always in hot water.

* * *

The god Thor was bored drinking mead in Valhalla and came down to earth. He met a chorus girl in Las Vegas, they climbed into bed and stayed there for three days and three nights. On leaving the fourth morning, he decided to tell her how she had been honored.

"My dear," he said, "I'm Thor!"

"You're Thor," said the girl, "I'm tho thore I can't even pith!"

He was making the final play now. "Honey, let me take you away from all this," he whispered. "Can't you picture the two of us: a little home in the country; a fireside; the patter of tiny feet in the nursery. And some day . . . some day . . ."

"Yes, yes," she urged, "go on!"

"And some day," he continued, "maybe we'll even get married."

* * *

Bert and Celia had gone together for some time. He had tried time after time to make love to her but to no avail. "I don't like it," she said.

One day, they were window-shopping and Celia saw a beautiful pair of red shoes. "Oh," she said, "I'd do anything for a pair of those pretty red shoes."

"You mean," said Bert, "that if I buy those shoes for you, you'd let me . . ."

"Yes," said Celia.

Bert bought the shoes. They drove out in the country, parked the car, and began making love. Celia twisted and wiggled with her legs high in the air.

"It's wonderful," exclaimed Bert. "But I thought you didn't like it."

"I don't," said Celia. "I'm only trying on my pretty red shoes!"

THE LINES LOVERS HAVE
HEARD MOST OFTEN

What makes you think I'm that kind of a girl?

Hands, hands, hands.

Can't we be just friends?

After that crummy dinner?

My mother would die if she found out.

And you say you're Harvey's best friend!

I had a feeling all evening you were leading up to this.

I'm not going to short change the man I marry.

Why is it every time I go out with a guy it ends up this way?

So that's why you kept making me have another drink.

This isn't the time nor the place.

I thought you would be different.

I'm really not in the mood.

Why me? You could get all the girls you want.

I'll hate myself in the morning.

I knew I couldn't trust you.

What'll my mother say when she goes through my diary?

But where? I hate going to motels.

Do we have to do the same thing *every* night?

41

Harry picked up a sexy-looking blonde at a bar, took her back to his car, and parked it in a dark alley. Now they were in the back seat making love for the third time. When they'd finished, before she could ask for more, Harry said, "Look, doll, I want to get a pack of cigarettes, I'll be right back!"

Down the street he ran into Mac, an old drinking buddy. "Hey, I've got a regular nympho in the back seat of my car," said Harry. "All you have to do is get in and go to work. It's all the same to this broad. She'll take anybody."

Mac found the car, opened the back door, groped around in the dark for the girl and in a minute the two of them were locked in embrace.

Five minutes later, a flashlight beam struck them in the face. "What are you two doing in there?" asked the cop.

"It's all right, officer," swallowed Mac, "this lady is my wife!"

"Oh, I'm sorry," said the cop. "I didn't know!"

"Neither did I," said Mac, "until you shined the flashlight in the car!"

* * *

THE MARRIEDS

Two secretaries were chatting at lunch. "I don't see," said the first, "what enjoyment you and your husband get out of going to a bar and getting tanked up every weekend."

"If you must know," said her friend, "every time he gets half lit, he thinks I'm somebody else's wife and sneaks me up to our apartment the back way!"

*   *   *

A wise woman is one who makes her husband feel as if he's head of the house when actually he's only chairman of the entertainment committee.

*   *   *

"I've been married four times. Do you think I'm a loose woman?"

"No, dearie. You're just a busy-body!"

"I'd like 25 yards of nylon for a night-gown," the woman told the clerk.

"You won't need that much material for a nightgown."

"I know. But my husband has more fun looking for it than finding it."

The pretty brunette kissed the fellow passionately at the airport passenger gate, then dashed aboard the waiting plane and burst into tears.

An elderly lady who had witnessed the scene was touched by the tenderness of it. She leaned over and patted the girl's shoulder. "Are you crying," asked the white-haired woman, "because you are leaving your husband?"

"No," sobbed the girl, "I'm crying because I'm going back to him."

* * *

SUSPICION

What you awaken in your wife when you come home from an out-of-town trip with new sex techniques.

* * *

Will: Do you cheat on your wife?
Bill: Who else?

* * *

Sam Wall, the popular Hollywood publicist, pleases pals with this poignant prank:

A newspaper offered five dollars for each published "Most Embarrassing Moment" contributed by a reader. Here's one they received:

I worked on the second shift at our

*plant. I got home an hour early last
night and found my wife with a
strange man. It was my most embarrassing moment.
Please send me ten dollars. The extra
five is for my wife 'cause she was
greatly embarrassed also."*

The editor sent fifteen dollars and this
note:
*Am enclosing another five dollars for
the strange man. I'm sure he was embarrassed, too!*

* * *

Sydney came home unexpectedly and
found his wife in the arms of the baker.

"I'm ashamed of you!" shrieked Sydney.
"Why are you making love to the baker
when it's the butcher we owe money to!"

* * *

Danny greeted Jack in the local tavern.
"Hey," said Danny, "your best friend is
up at your apartment right now making
love to your wife."

"What?" screamed Jack, as he flew out
the door. "I'll kill that bastard!"

Three minutes later, he returned to the
barroom. "Say," he said to Danny, "you
made me run up a whole flight of stairs
for nothing. Telling me my best friend
was making love to my wife. I never saw
that guy before in my life."

47

"This suit was a surprise from my wife."

"Really?"

"Yeah. I came home unexpectedly one night and there it was—right on the back of a chair."

* * *

Coming home at a quarter of three,
I caught my wife cheating on me,
    I raged, "Who's this fink?"
    She cried, like a wink,
"I don't know—it's a new one on me!"

* * *

"Boy, do I have an absent-minded milkman," announced Henry to his pal Pete. "This morning, my wife Charlotte wasn't feeling too well, so I stayed home a little longer to take care of her. All of a sudden I hear the milkman at the back door. I'm not dressed, so I grabbed the nearest thing—Charlotte's bathrobe—throw it around me, and I answer the knock."

"So?" asked Tom.

"So this nut grabs me in his arms and starts hugging and kissing me!"

"So?"

"So, can you imagine the coincidence? The milkman's wife must have a bathrobe just like Charlotte's!"

48

George Johnston, Totie Fields' musical conductor (and husband) breaks up buddies with this bauble:

The hungover couple were having late afternoon breakfast after an extremely wild all-night party held in the Park Avenue penthouse.

"Sweetheart, this is a little embarrassing," said the husband, "but was it you I made love to in the den last night?"

"About what time?" asked his wife.

* * *

RECREATION
Making love with your wife even though she's already pregnant

* * *

Dougherty came home late one night a trifle "under the weather." Since he couldn't find the key to the front door he began climbing through the window. He was almost inside when a policeman stopped him.

"Sure this is my house!" Dougherty blubbered, pulling the cop in after him. "This is my hall, that's my carpet, this is my bedroom, that's my bed, that's my wife, and you see that guy in bed with her? That's me!"

Goofy George and his bowling buddy Ken were relaxing with a few brews. "I came home last night," said George, "and I found my wife sitting on the couch in the parlor making love to some other guy."

"No kiddin'?" said Ken. 'I hope you knew how to handle it!"

"I sure did! I fixed them, all right. I turned out the light so they couldn't see what they were doing!"

* * *

Paul stopped by his friend's house to visit but he wasn't in. The wife insisted he stay for coffee, and after a little idle chatter, she said, "I have to warn you, my husband'll be home in another hour!"

"But I haven't done anything wrong!" Paul protested.

"That's true," she said, "I just wanted you to know you have only an hour in case you decided to."

* * *

Mr. Green came home with a carton of ice cream. "You want me to dish you up some ice cream, dear?" he asked his wife.

"About how hard is it?" she asked.

"About as hard as *you know what*," he laughed.

"In that case, *pour me some*," said Mrs. Green.

Husband: Honey, my new suit has a 14-inch zipper.

Wife: So what? When the guy next door opens up his two big garage doors out comes his son's tricycle.

* * *

Rudy returned from a selling trip to discover that his wife had been unfaithful to him. "Who was it?" he demanded. "Was it my friend, Lloyd?"

"No!" snapped his wife.

"Was it my buddy, Barry?"

"No!"

"Then it must've been my pal, Mort?"

"What's the matter?" she screamed. "Don't you think I have any friends of my own?"

* * *

Jane was fuming as she burst into her neighbor's house. "I'm so mad at Arnold," she cried, "I don't know what to do!"

"Why?" said her friend.

"Last night I dreamed some blonde hussy was flirting with him, and he was purring like a kitten."

"Now, Jane, it was only a dream!"

"I know, but if he acts like that in *my* dreams, what in the world do you suppose he does in *his?*"

51

A husband and wife were asleep. About 3 A.M. the wife dreamed of secretly meeting another man. Then she dreamed she saw her husband coming. So in her sleep she screamed, "Good heavens! It's my husband!"

Her husband woke up, leaped from the bed, and jumped out the window!

* * *

DON JUAN'S ADVICE
Love thy neighbor all through the day,
But first make sure her husband's
away.

* * *

Most husbands never stop being romantic, but they sure catch hell every time their wives find out.

* * *

There once was a man in his prime,
Who lived with three wives at one time.
   When asked, "Why the third?"
   He replied, "One's absurd,
And bigamy, sir, is a crime!"

* * *

The young married couple lived right across the street from a beautiful widow. Whenever the husband ran over to borrow

52

anything, which was often, it took him longer than the wife thought it should. Exasperated by a half-hour quest for ice cubes, the wife telephoned. After a considerable delay, the widow answered.

"I'd like to know," snapped the jealous wife, "why it takes my husband so long to get something over there!"

"So would I," said the widow. "And this interruption isn't helping any."

* * *

Did you hear about the man on the flying trapeze who caught his wife in the act?

* * *

Hank: How did you get the black eye?
Frank: Our new maid is ticklish.
Hank: Did she sock you?
Frank: No. My wife did when she heard the maid giggle.

* * *

Motion picture producer-director, Dennis Kane, tells about the woman who gave her husband a little kiss on the back of his bald head. He was so shocked, he dropped his newspaper. "That's the second time you've kissed me in four months, dear!"

"But, darling," she sighed. "I thought you *wanted* me to show a little more interest in the physical side of marriage."

Augie came home unexpectedly and found his wife in bed with a naked man. He pulled a pistol out of the dresser drawer and was about to shoot when his wife pleaded, "Don't, don't! Who do you think bought us that house in the country, that beautiful Cadillac, my mink coat?"

"Are *you* the man?" asked Augie.

The naked lover nodded.

"Then cover yourself with the blanket." said Augie. "You wanna catch cold?"

Love is such a beautiful thing. It's a shame people have to get married and spoil it.

* * *

A man walked into a store to buy a brassiere for his wife. "What size?" asked the salesgirl.

"I'm not sure," answered the husband.

"All right," said the clerk, "Is she a grapefruit?"

"No," he said.

"Is she an orange?"

"No."

"Perhaps she's an egg."

"That's it!" said the man. "An egg. Fried."

* * *

The young husband watched his flat-chested wife as she tried on her new brassiere.

"What did you buy that for?" he asked. "You haven't got anything to put in it."

"Listen," said his wife icily. "Do I complain about your wearing shorts?"

* * *

OPTIMIST

A man who thinks his wife has quit smoking cigarettes when he finds cigar butts in the house

Cliff Huseby of California Business Mc-chines likes the one about the couple who had been married 40 years. They decided to have a second honeymoon and do everything exactly as on their first. When they got back, the husband was asked by a friend how the second honeymoon came out.

"Well," replied the dejected gent, "we took the same train to the same town, went to the same hotel, and got the same room. Everything exactly as we did on our original honeymoon—except one thing. This time *I* went into the bathroom and cried."

* * *

Jeanne: Tomorrow is our fiftieth wedding anniversary. What shall we do?
John: Let's celibate!

* * *

Mr. and Mrs. Garvey checked into a motel and asked for the best accommodations. The clerk recommended the bridal suite.

"Why the bridal suite?" asked Mr. Garvey. "My wife and I have been married for five years!"

"Look," said the clerk, "if I let you have the main ballroom, that doesn't mean you have to dance, does it?"

Andrew and Lillian were airing their marital troubles in court.

"We were very happy for a couple of years, your honor," sobbed Lillian, "and then the baby came."

"Hmmm," sympathized the Judge. "Was the baby a boy or a girl?"

"A girl, of course," snapped the wife. "And she moved in next door!"

* * *

MALE MENOPAUSE
Change of wife

* * *

A real sexy-looking dish walked into a lawyer's office and said, "I wanna divorce my husband."

"On what grounds?" asked the attorney.

"Infidelity," answered the woman. "I don't think my husband has been faithful to me."

"What makes you think that?"

"Well," said the sexpot, "I don't think he's the father of my child."

* * *

The defense lawyer was bearing down hard. "You say," he sneered, "that my client came at you with a broken bottle in his hand. But didn't you have something in your hand?"

"Yes," said the plaintiff, "his wife. She's okay in bed, but not as good as a broken bottle in a fight."

* * *

"Your honor," she told the judge, "I want a divorce. My husband has been cheating on me."

"Do you have any evidence to support this claim of your husband's infidelity?"

"Yes, sir. Just last night I was walking down Broadway when I saw him go into a movie with another woman."

"Who was this other woman?" asked the judge.

"I don't know. I never saw her before."

"Then why didn't you follow them into the theater and find out who she was. It may have been just a harmless coincidence. You should have gone in after them."

"I would have," she explained, "but the fellow I was with had already seen the picture."

* * *

COUPLE MAKING LOVE
Husband: Did I hurt you?
Wife: No, why?
Husband: You moved!

Their marriage had ended in the divorce court, deluged with hard feelings. Now, a year later, they happened to meet at a cocktail party. After both had had a few martinis, he put his arm around her shoulder. "Hey, honey," he said, "for old time's sake, let's go to bed!"

"Over my dead body!" she snapped.

"Nothing has changed, has it?" he sneered.

* * *

George Claire, Pittsburgh's premier theatrical agent, overheard two psychiatrists talking: "Anything unusual come in this week?" asked the first.

"I'll say," replied the second. "I've got a woman patient who hates her husband so much she closes her eyes during lovemaking. She doesn't want to see him enjoying himself."

* * *

"How did you get so banged up?" the doctor asked his patient as he applied the iodine.

"It was all a mistake, doc," replied the man. "I came home drunk last night. And while I was making love to my wife, I got so carried away, I said, 'Honey, you're almost as good as my wife.'"

The squeaking of bedsprings increased in intensity. Then, silence. Her quiet voice broke the stillness of the darkened room.

"I'm not myself tonight," she insisted.

"Well, whoever you are," he sighed, "it certainly is an improvement."

* * *

Edgar and Dave were on their way home from playing poker late one night. "I'm always afraid when I come home late from a game," said Edgar. "I shut off the engine of my car half a block from the house and coast into the garage. I take off my shoes and sneak upstairs. I'm as quiet as possible, but just when I settle down into bed, my wife sits up and starts hollering at me."

"You got the wrong technique" said Dave. "I never have no trouble. I barge into the garage, slam the door, stomp into the house, and make a hell of a racket. I go upstairs to the bedroom, pat my wife and say, 'Hey, baby, how about it?' You know what? She always pretends she's asleep!"

* * *

"How is it I find you making love to the cook?" asked his wife.

"I don't know," he said, "unless it's because you're wearing sneakers."

61

Robert entered the bedroom, undressed quickly, and crawled into bed. He leaned over and kissed his wife on the cheek. Then he waited a moment and gave her a resounding wallop on the behind.

"What's that for?" she shrieked, jumping up in bed.

"For not opening your eyes to see who it was!"

*   *   *

Septuagenarian Simon ogled all the young females who came within range of his weak vision.

"Don't you notice how your husband eyes all the girls?" asked a neighbor of Simon's wife.

"Oh, yes," she answered, quite undisturbed. "But he's like a deep-sea diver with an itchy nose. He feels it but he can't get at it."

*   *   *

The couple were visiting a rancher friend who was boasting that his prize bull "serviced" about a cow a day, six days a week.

"There!" said the wife scornfully to her husband. "Five or six times a week is nothing to a real champion!"

"Yeah," sighed the weary husband, "but don't forget, the bull never has the same cow twice!"

"How's married life, Lucille?" asked a girlfriend.

"Not bad," she replied, "considering it now takes Harold all night to do what he used to do all night."

*   *   *

Man lives a terrible life. When he's single, the girls convince him he should get married.

When he's married his wife convinces him he should've stayed single.

If he doesn't bring her flowers, she gets mad.

If he does bring her flowers, she gets suspicious.

If he comes home early, she thinks he wants something.

If he comes home late, she thinks he's already had it.

*   *   *

Husband: I have never had an affair in my whole life. Can you say the same?

Wife: Yes. But not with such a straight face.

*   *   *

FRENCH PHILOSOPHY

Wives, take care! If you try too hard to wear the pants around your house, you are liable to find your husband has located a girlfriend who doesn't wear any.

George Zell, president of Colave, the California sportswear firm, tells visiting buyers this beaut:

A wealthy dress manufacturer went to Italy to buy new fabrics for his fall line. Upon his arrival in Rome he became an instant Casanova, spending lavishly on the Latin ladies.

When his wife heard about his adventures in *amore*, she cabled him: COME HOME. STOP SPENDING MONEY FOR WHAT YOU CAN GET HERE FOR FREE.

He wired her back: PHOOEY ON YOU AND YOUR BARGAINS.

* * *

"If I ever get married," Noel told his buddy Jerome, "I want a girl who is a lady in the living room, an economist in the kitchen, and a witch in the bedroom."

Six months later they met again.

"I got married," announced Noel.

"Great!" said Jerome. "Did you get what you wanted?"

"Yeah, but it's a little turned around," admitted Noel. "The girl I married is a witch in the living room, a lady in the kitchen, and an economist in the bedroom."

* * *

MISTRESS
Something between a mister and a mattress

Charlie had been cheating on his wife for years. One night he arrived home in the wee hours, crept into the bedroom, and began undressing. His wife, who'd been watching him out of the corner of her eye, cried, "Charlie! Where's your underwear?"

"My God!" he exclaimed. "I've been robbed!"

* * *

Waldo was given to going out frequently at night and leaving his wife alone. As he strutted out the door, he would rub more salt into the wound by his farewell: "Good night, mother of three!"

One evening Waldo's wife decided she had had enough of this, and when he grabbed his hat and said, "Good night, mother of three!" she replied, "Good night, father of one!"

Now Waldo stays at home.

* * *

A little boy at the zoo with his parents stared at the elephant with the enormous erection. "What's that?" he asked his mother.

"It's nothing!" she replied. "Shhhh!"

The boy then asked his father, who answered, "Why don't you ask your mother?"

"I did ask her and she said it's nothing!"

"Well," said the father, "she's been spoiled!"

Fairlawn, New Jersey, housewife, Mimi Marks, relates this rousing saga of suburban society:

Sol wanted to do away with his wife. Arsenic seemed the best way. "Don't poison her," advised a friend. "If you want to kill her, keep her up late, make love to her every night, and I guarantee you in thirty days she'll be dead!"

Sol followed his friend's advice. He kept his wife up till three o'clock every morning and made violent love to her several times a night, knowing that she would die in just thirty days.

Exactly twenty-five days later, Sol's spouse was seen singing and whooping it up at a local gin mill. Sol had lost 42 pounds! He was at home in a wheelchair, only a quivering shadow of a man.

A neighbor walked in the house and told him about his wife's carrying on. "It's all right," said Sol smiling. "Let the crazy dame have a good time. She doesn't know that she's only got five more days to live!"

She's only got five more days to live!

67

Billy Marvin, Los Angeles' top rock group booker, came up with this biting bit of banter:

They had met at a bar. She was the mother of seven kids and divorced. He was still married. After several drinks they adjourned to a motel. When the passion had subsided, he asked, "How was it?"

"It was all right, but I can't say I thought much of your organ."

"Of course," he said, "I didn't expect to play in an auditorium!"

* * *

THE PARTING

Burlesque did much to popularize a form of comedy known as the sketch. Probably the most widely played of these was this little dramatization:

(*The scene is a small living room. The wife sits on the couch as the husband dons his hat and coat. He picks up his portfolio and goes to the door.*)

Husband: Well, goodbye, dear. I'll be gone for two weeks. (*He exits.*)

Wife: I thought he'd never go. (*Just then the lover enters from the kitchen.*)

Lover (*furtively*) : Has he gone?

Wife: Yes, for two whole weeks.

Lover: Darling!

Wife: Sweetheart! (*They embrace. Suddenly we hear fumbling of a key in the lock of the door.*)

Wife: Oh, Richard, darling, it must be my husband. He mustn't find you here.

Lover: Where can I hide?

Wife: Quick, Richard, into the closet. (*Richard hurriedly hides in the closet and the wife regains her seat on the couch as the husband enters.*)

Husband: Hello, dear.

Wife (*nervously*): What are you doing back so soon?

Husband: I forgot some papers (*He goes to the bureau and stuffs some papers into his portfolio.*)

Wife: Make sure you don't forget anything else.

Husband: I won't. (*He goes to the door, turns, and says*) Goodbye, dear. (*He is about to leave when he remembers something. He walks to the closet and knocks on the door.*) Goodbye Richard. Take care of yourself! (*He exits.*)

BLACKOUT

* * *

ADULTERY
Two wrong people doing the right thing

* * *

"How's your sex life, Irene?"

"When I first married my husband, every night it was the Eiffel Tower. Now it's the Leaning Tower of Pisa once a month.

69

Niles met Patti, a married woman, at a party. After a little chitchat he propositioned her. She thought it over and figured it would be an easy way to make some side money without her husband knowing it. So Patti made a date for Niles to come to her house when her husband was at work.

Niles kept the date, and enjoyed himself. Just before leaving the house, he placed a twenty-dollar bill on the end of the table.

Later that day when Patti's hubby came home, he saw the twenty-dollar bill. "Was Niles here today?" he asked.

Thinking she had been caught, Patti decided it would be best to tell the truth. "Yes," she gasped.

"Niles is an all right guy," said her husband. "He borrowed twenty dollars from me at the party and damned if he didn't pay me back the same day he said he would."

*   *   *

SEVENTH COMMANDMENT
(SUBURBAN VERSION)
Thou shalt not omit adultery.

*   *   *

Patsy lay in the hospital bed, his left leg precariously perched in a pulley system, his right arm swathed from wrist to shoulder in a plastar of Paris cast, and his face covered with bandages. His buddy Louie stood at his bedside.

"How did it happen?" asked Louie.

"You know that cute married broad who just moved in next door to me?" asked Patsy, "Well, I was having a ball making it with her last night about midnight when her husband came home and caught me."

"Well," said Louie, "it could've been worse."

"Are you kidding? The guy almost killed me. What do you mean, it could've been worse?"

"If he'd came home an hour earlier, he would've caught me!"

* * *

Morris was out in back of his house trying to fly a kite for his kid. Nothing happened. The thing just refused to stay in the air. Suddenly, his wife appeared. "You're an idiot," she said. "Don't you know you've got to hang a piece of tail on the end of the kite?"

"I don't understand you," said Morris. "Last night I asked you for a piece of tail and you told me to go fly a kite!"

71

Joe Bolker, California's leading contributor to the arts, made this delightful contribution:

"Doc," said Smithers, "I don't know what's the matter with me. I feel rotten all the time."

"It's quite simple," said the physician. "You're frustrated. Next time you get the urge, no matter where you are, grab your wife and have sex with her. You'll see how much better you'll feel."

It seemed reasonable. Smithers went home and returned the next day to thank the doctor.

"Worked wonders!" he confided. "Did just what you told me. Walked into the house, grabbed my wife, threw her on the living room floor, and we went right at it. And now I feel like a new man!"

"Did your wife mind?" inquired the M.D.

"She kind of enjoyed it!" said Smithers. "But I don't think her bridge club will ever come back to our house again!"

I don't think her bridge club will ever
come back again!"

Buck Owens, the great country music star, told this one to pals at his Bakersfield Charity Golf Tournament:

"Doc, lotsa times I git the matin' urge out in the fields," confessed farmer Jackson. "But there's no way to let my wife know 'cause she spends her day back around the barn. Then when the day's plowin' is done, me and the missus are jest too tired. Well, you might say our happy marriage ain't too satisfyin' lately. I was hopin' you could help."

"Of course," advised the doctor. "Just take a shotgun with you into the fields. Then when you get the urge, shoot the gun off as a signal to Mrs. Jackson to come-a-runnin'."

The farmer went home and told the plan to his wife. Two weeks later, he returned, unhappier than ever. "It's muh woman," he cried. "She done died."

"What happened?" asked the doctor.

"We done forget it was squirrel-huntin' season," he moaned. "The pore woman jest run herself to death answerin' all them gunshots."

*   *   *

THE OTHERS

The day after the wedding the bride walked into her home alone. "What happened?" asked her shocked mother.

"Last night, we got to the hotel all right," explained the bride tearfully. "We were up in the room. He took off all my clothes. Then he took off all his clothes. Then he put on my clothes. And I haven't seen him since!"

* * *

College boy: I think my roommate Bob is becoming a queer.
His father: How can you tell?
College boy: Well, he closes his eyes now every time I kiss him.

* * *

Did you hear about the impressionable young lad who moved to Greenwich Village and turned prematurely gay?

HOMOSEXUAL
A man's man

*   *   *

Male nurses are generally known for their efficiency. Nurse Nicholas is one of the best. He can make a patient without disturbing the bed.

*   *   *

A Hollywood lawyer is building a big reputation in the movie colony because of his success in handling delicate cases. His latest one involved a prominent motion picture actor who was arrested on charges of sodomy.

The lawyer got the charge reduced to tail-gating.

*   *   *

Comedy actor Joey Forman told me this one at a birthday party for Bill Dana:

Boniface was standing near the edge of a lake when his roommate Horace began shouting, "Help! Help!"

"Wait!" yelled Boniface, "I'll throw you a buoy!"

"Don't fool around." cried Horace. "I'm really drowning!"

76

Wallace was so terribly depressed he actually wanted to kill himself. "I'm a loser. I fail at everything," he said to his roommate. "I'm going to end it all!"

"You mustn't give up" implored his lover. "Have you prayed to the Lord?"

"No."

"Then you must pray to God! *She'll* help you!"

* * *

Percival and Thaddeus went to a mortuary. "When we die, we'd like to be buried together in the same coffin," said Percival to the Funeral Director.

"I'm sorry," he replied, "but we couldn't possibly do anything like that!"

"You could put us face to face, side to side, or back to back," said Thaddeus.

"We can't do it. The best we could do is cremate you and—"

"Put us in an urn?"

"No, a fruit jar!" said the undertaker.

* * *

Stranded actor: Is it true you can telegraph flowers anywhere?

Telegraph operator: Yes!

Stranded actor: Then telegraph me back to New York. I'm a pansy.

The restaurant owner was considering hiring a bartender with a dubious work record. He had been fired from three previous bartending jobs—the first for having his hand in the till, the second for constantly coming to work late and the third when his boss discovered he was gay.

Turning to his prospective employee, the man said, "You'd better not be one cent short, and you'd better get here right on time every day . . . Now kiss me and go to work!"

* * *

GAY RANCHERO
A cowhand who rides sidesaddle

* * *

A fairy fellow was beating up a tipsy truck driver because the trucker had made snide remarks about his sexuality. Just then two of the homo's companions passed by.

"Isn't that Francis thrashing that poor man?"

"Yes," said the other fag. "Like I always say, once a tomboy, always a tomboy."

* * *

CLOSET QUEEN
A male fraud

If horse-racing is the sport of kings, is drag-racing the sport of queens?"

*   *   *

At basic training the sergeant shouted at the lined-up recruits, "Count off!"

"One!" "Two!" "Three!" "Four!" came from distinct voices.

The next man in line daintily pursed his lips and whispered very softly, "One."

"Hey, you!" bellowed the sergeant. "Are you one?"

"Yeth!" lisped the recruit. "Are you *one*, too?"

*   *   *

Only seven people survived the shipwreck and landed on a desert island. Six women and a man. One problem was solved right away. The girls agreed to share the lone male. Each woman would spend one night with him. Sundays he would recuperate.

This arrangement continued for three exhausting months. One Sabbath morning, our hero was relaxing on the sand when he spotted a raft offshore with a fellow on it. Overjoyed at finding this unexpected help, he ran to the water's edge and shouted, "Hello, there!"

The figure on the float stood up, waved a lacy handkerchief, and lisped, "Hi, sssweetheart!"

"Oh, my God!" moaned the Island Prince. "There go my Sundays!"

John Barbour, the controversial and uproariously funny movie critic, came up with this clever bit of persiflage:

Two knights, resplendent in shining armor and mounted on handsome steeds, rode through the forest followed by their faithful little page, who was huddled uncomfortably on his burro.

As they arrived at a strange castle surrounded by the usual moat, one knight shouted the traditional "Tallyho" to inform the castle's owners that the travelers desired lodging for the night.

The drawbridge was soon lowered, and out tiptoed a man dressed in flowing robes of many colors. "So," he lisped, with a hand perched on his hip. "What can I do for you fellows?"

The tired knights, anxious for lodging but taken aback by their limp-wristed host, looked at each other in dismay. Then one whispered to the other, "Promise him anything, but give him our page."

A couple stopped at a gas station for towing information.

"Say, mister," asked the husband of the attendant. "Can you tell us where Ferryville is?"

"Gee, I don't know," said the man. "Let me ask my wife. Hey, Charles!"

*   *   *

Did you hear about the dour college choir girls who were sleeping together?

Two of them were playing hymns.

*   *   *

A suburban mother was arranging the table for a formal party when her daughter walked in and announced dramatically, "Mother, I'm a Lesbian!"

"So, go upstairs and shave!"

*   *   *

MacDonald just got a promotion, and he strode into a downtown bar to celebrate. "Gimme a whiskey sour," he said to the bartender. "And give that guy at the end of the bar a drink, too!"

When MacDonald finished his whiskey sour, he called, "I'll take another one! This time leave the fruit out of it!"

"You brute!" screamed the man at the end of the bar, "I didn't ask for a drink in the first place."

Vic sat down next to a girl at a bar. He bought her a drink and began coming on strong. "Look," she said, "before we go too far I just want you to know that I'm a Lesbian!"

"That's okay," said Vic. "I've got a cousin in Beirut."

* * *

LESBIAN
A mannish depressive with illusions of gender

* * *

Didja hear about the limp-wristed lad who cut himself while shaving?

Gads! Were his legs a mess!

* * *

A big brute of a man walked into a bar and in a booming voice shouted, "Gimme a fifth of whiskey."

The bartender handed the Goliath a fresh fifth, which the man placed to his lips and drained dry. When the last was gone, he beat his fists on his great chest and roared, "There! I feel like a bull!"

From the other end of the bar a voice implored, "Mooooooo . . . !"

Simon was telling Ashley about his unusual experience that afternoon. "There I was on the corner of Hollywood and Vine when this movie star stopped her car and offered me a lift."

"Then, wouldn't you know it, she took me to a hotel, undressed immediately and told me I could have anything I wanted. So I took the car."

"And you did right," said Ashley. "Her clothes would never have fit you."

* * *

"I hear that in college you won the Golden Gloves," said Giles to the man standing beside him at a bar.

"Yeth!" he answered, "and they came all the way up to my elbowth!"

* * *

The Gay Liberation Movement in America announced its platform: "We want our own place to live and a chance to elect our own Mayor, Sheriff, and Homecoming Queen."

* * *

ROMAN QUEER
Gladiatum

A couple from Cleveland were touring Manhattan. While they were strolling through Greenwich Village, the woman's eyes grew wider and wider in amazement and shock. She turned to her husband and said, "They ought to take all these fairies and put them all on an island!"

"Dear," said the man. "They already did and we're on it!"

*   *   *

Did you hear about the gay guy who was so ugly he had to go out with girls?

*   *   *

Jesse James once got rattled while robbing a train with his gang. "Line up against the wall," shouted Jesse. "We're gonna screw all the men and rob all the women!"

"Wait a minute, Jesse," said one of his henchmen, "ain't you got that backwards?"

"Now ju*th* hold on there," shouted a voice from the back. "You heard what Mi*th*ter Jame*th th*aid!"

Personable music publisher Lucky Carle told this pearl at the last record producers convention:

Ambrose and Peri, who had been living together in conjugal bliss for years, suddenly decided they just couldn't stand being with one another any more. They agreed to split their household possessions and go their separate ways.

In divvying up their worldly treasures, they got into an argument over who owned a certain chartreuse and hot pink necktie.

"Stop this arguing at once," sputtered Ambrose. "I'm simply bushed from all our quarreling, and now you're doing me in by saying this is your tie."

"Well, pooh, pooh!" goaded Peri. "As if you have a priority on being tired. How do you think I feel after all we've meant to each other? Give me back my tie!"

"I won't! I won't!" squealed Ambrose.

The verbal battle continued for hours until finally, Peri broke. "All right, if you want to be mean and spiteful, take the wretched old tie, and you know what you can do with it!"

"Oh, so now you want to make up!"

*   *   *

THE PROS

Milly and Alice had come from the sticks to storm New York together, but things didn't work out so well and they lost track of one another for some time. Finally, the two of them, both looking rather prosperous now, met on Broadway. Milly asked Alice what she was doing with herself.

"I've got a wonderful job," replied Alice. "I arrive just in time for the boss to take me out to lunch, then we generally go to the races or a ball game, then dinner, a show, and a quiet little snack at a chic supper club. What are you doing?"

"Funny thing," said Milly, "I'm a call girl, too!"

*   *   *

MINUTE MAN
A man who double parks in front of a house of ill-repute

A gorgeous babe, formerly employed as an usherette in a theater, went into the oldest profession. The money was better, and besides she really loved the life.

But now, as her customers leave, from force of habit she says, "Please do not reveal the ending to the others waiting ..."

* * *

HEIGHT OF PRESUMPTION
The call girl who lists herself in the phone book under "public relations"

* * *

"I'll never do it that way!" shouted the call girl as she slammed the door and raced down stairs into the lobby of the shabby hotel.

"Don't take it so hard, Myrtle," said the night clerk, who had heard her outburst. "Some guys are just weirdos. How did he want you to do it?"

"On the cuff!" said Myrtle.

* * *

Wanting to please all types of customers with a variety of girls, an enterprising madam set up a three-story house of sport. She had ex-secretaries, selected for their efficiency, on the first floor; ex-models, selected for their beauty, on the second; and ex-schoolteachers, selected for their intelligence, on the third floor.

As time went on, the madam noticed that almost all the play went to the third floor. One day, she stopped a steady customer and asked him why.

"You know how those schoolteachers are," said the man. "They make you do it over and over, until you get it right!"

* * *

PRAYER OF THE DESTITUTE PROSTITUTE
Now I lay me down too cheap.

* * *

"Absolutely not, Mr. Grant," said the call girl to one of her regular customers. "No more credit. You're into me for too much already."

* * *

CALL GIRL'S CALLING CARD
The main ingredient of spice
Is variety in your vice.
So add a little to your diet
Even *if you have to* buy *it!*

* * *

Then there was the brothel-keeper who was determined not to let the government know how much money she was making. So she kept a separate set of towels.

Harriet and Milton were on their honeymoon in Hawaii. Milton sat amazed by the pool watching his beautiful wife churn up the water. When she got out, he asked, "Honey, where did you learn to be such a great swimmer?"

"Didn't you know?" explained Harriet. "I used to be a streetwalker in Venice!"

* * *

HONOLULU HOOKER'S SLOGAN
It's a business to do pleasure with you.

* * *

Frank Bresee, America's acknowledged authority on nostalgic radio comedy shows, came up with this dilly:

Gloria and Joan, two New York City call girls, walked into a cocktail lounge and sat at the bar. Without being asked, the bar-jockey served them their favorite brands of beer. "How'd you know what we wanted?" inquired Gloria.

"Aw, I'm just a smart bartender," he replied.

"Baloney!" said Joan. "You just guessed!"

"Oh, yeah? See that guy who just came in? He'll want a scotch on the rocks. Now watch, I'll ask him."

Sure enough, the new customer ordered scotch over ice. The girls were astonished.

As the barman passed them once again, he winked and said, "Smart bartender! You'd better believe it!"

A while later, the bartender leaned over the bar toward the ladies of the evening. "Look," he asked confidentially, "I've always wanted to ask this question. Do prostitutes ever get pregnant?"

"Certainly we do!" snapped Gloria. "Where do you think smart bartenders come from?"

*　　*　　*

A senior citizen walked into a house of ill-repute and said to the madam, "How much?"

"Forty dollars!" replied the woman.

"You're putting me on!" said the old man.

"That'll be ten dollars extra!" added the madam.

*　　*　　*

"If I'm not in bed by ten o'clock," said one female barfly to the other, "I'm going home!"

*　　*　　*

Girls can go out and give it away,
But they'll be arrested if they do it for pay.

91

When the prostitute died, her co-workers gathered at the funeral parlor to pay their respects. A friend got up to say a few words:

"Carol was a wonderful girl. She was kind, she loved animals, she gave to charity..."

"You see," said one old pro to another, "no matter what profession you're in, you gotta die before they'll say a few nice words about you."

* * *

PROSTITUTION
Fee love

* * *

Ernie paid a visit to a party girl establishment and had a grand time with three of the prettiest dolls he'd ever seen. When he asked the lady who ran the place for the bill, she said, "there's no charge! And thank you!"

Ernie was astounded. A week later he came back with a friend who was really hopped up over this freeloading bonanza. They had their fill of the harem of lovely ladies and started to leave. The madam met them at the door and presented them with a staggering bill.

"I don't get it," said Ernie. "Last week the whole thing didn't cost a dime and now you're asking an arm and a leg. What gives?"

"This week," said the madam, "you pay our regular price. Last week they were filming movies!"

* * *

PROFESSIONAL
A girl who takes it in her head to make money

* * *

Long a favorite in one of the plushest establishments, Mitzi suddenly announced to the madam that she was going to leave.

"But, Mitzi," protested her employer, "you're one of our best girls! You are making a lot of money. You were upstairs thirty times last night!"

"That's just it," complained Mitzi. "My feet are killing me!"

* * *

Madam Gibbs and Madam Moss were talking shop. "It was awful," lamented Madam Gibbs. "I had a fire at my place."

"Didn't you call the firemen?" asked Madam Moss.

"That's what made it so awful," groaned the first lady. "It took the firemen two hours to put the fire out, and it took my girls two days to put the firemen out!"

A traveling salesman driving through the back roads saw a sign: *Grandma's Bawdy House—5 miles*. He drove on and in a few moments saw: *Grandma's Bawdy House—3 miles*.

As he got closer to the town, his urge began to grow, and by the time he pulled up in front of *Grandma's Bawdy House*, he was ready.

The salesman knocked on the door. A voice said, "Come in!" A little old lady sat in a rocking chair knitting. "I'd like to take advantage of your hospitality, grandma!" said the traveling man.

"That'll be fifty dollars!" said the white-haired woman. "Right through that door!"

The salesman forked over the money, crashed through the door, and found himself outside the house. Then staring him in the face stood another sign that read: *You've Just Been Screwed by Grandma.*

A beautiful, incredibly well-built, and very young blonde strolled up Park Avenue one evening throwing come-hither glances at the men she passed. A guy fell in stride with her. "Do I get the impression you're looking to do business?" he asked, staring at her perfectly formed figure.

"Yeah," said the beauty, "you get the impression."

"How much?" he asked.

"One hundred for the night," she said, parting her voluptuous lips.

"One hundred dollars?" he gasped. "Why so much?"

"The center cut always costs more!" she smiled.

*   *   *

ITINERANT HOOKER
A New York girl who flies down to Miami every so often for a little change

*   *   *

Emma, aged 80, opened up a house of ill-repute right across the street from one operated by two established pros. Within a week, the old woman had taken away 50 percent of their business. In a month, it was almost all gone. The prosties decided to find out why.

They marched across the street and confronted the white-haired dowager. "What the hell are you doin' over here that's takin' away all our business?"

"I'll tell you," said the octogenarian. "When I was a young girl, I used to give it away. Then I got smart and sold it for fifty bucks a throw. Now, I'm buying it all back!"

* * *

From 1920 through 1945, Polly Adler ran a bordello in New York. She was considered the most highly publicized procuress of her time. Here's a story she often related to friends:

Three thugs decided to pull a heist at Polly's establishment. They broke into the house and one made for Polly's office to get the receipts; the second leveled a gun at the assembled menfolk; and the third robber led all the girls into one of the bedrooms where he ordered them down on the floor.

Wisely following the command, the girls hurriedly stretched themselves out on the floor, facing the ceiling.

"Turn over!" growled the gunman. "We came here to rob the joint, not to patronize it!"

* * *

ONE-ACT PLAY

(*The phone rings in the brothel and the madam answers it*)

Madam: Hello. This is Madam Pandora speaking!

Voice on the Phone: Operator? I asked for the *Poor* House!

San Francisco ladies of the evening have formed an organization called Coyote. Comedian Vaughn Meader told this one at their annual Hookers Ball:

Bert, staying at a hotel for one night, said to the bellboy, "Can you get me a prostitute?"

"Sure," said the boy.

"I want the tallest, skinniest whore in the world!" demanded Bert.

"Don't worry," said the hotel employee. "I know just the gal."

Thirty minutes later, there was a knock on Bert's door and in walked a six-foot-two woman who weighed all of seventy-nine pounds. Bert told her to undress. She did. Then he told her to get down on her hands and knees. She obeyed.

Bert then went to a closet, opened the door, and led out a gigantic Great Dane. He brought the dog to the skinny, kneeling call girl and pointed to her. "Now see," said Bert to the dog, "that's just what you're going to look like if you don't eat your Gravy Train!"

*   *   *

Have you heard about the new instrument of credit created especially for bawdy houses?

It's called a *Bangamericard.*

Three girls had been arrested for streetwalking and arraigned in night court. When the judge demanded an explanation from the first woman, she said, "I'm a nightclub hat-check girl and I was just walking home!"

When he questioned the second young thing, she gave him the same answer. Turning to the third, he said, "And I suppose you're a hat-check girl, too?"

"No, your honor," she confessed. "I'm a prostitute."

"Really?" said the judge, smiling. "How's business these nights?"

"Lousy," retorted the pro, "what with all these hat-check girls around."

*　　*　　*

A prostie wasn't feeling well so she went to the doctor. After an examination, the M.D. said to her, "Take these pills and stay out of bed for three days!"

*　　*　　*

Hear about the $100 a night call girl working the Minneapolis/St. Paul area? Customers call her the tail of two cities.

Two drunks were sitting in a cocktail lounge. "Say," said the first one, noticing a young lady seated at the other end of the bar, "isn't that Hortense?"

"I don't know," shrugged this friend. "She looks relaxed to me."

*   *   *

Then there was the prospective client who was extremely chagrined as he critically appraised his girl for the night.

"Girl?" he barked. "Girl? You must must have spent your girlhood entertaining George Washington's troops!"

"Please!" protested the veteran prostitute. "Remember, mine is the oldest profession."

"Yeah," he moaned, "but I'll be damned if I'm gonna spend the night with a charter member!"

*   *   *

LA DOLCE VITA
A streetwalker in Rome who believes in never letting a Dago by

*   *   *

"You are charged," said the judge, "with the serious offense of assault and battery on your husband. How do you plead?"

"Innocent," said the shapely defendant. "I hit him because he called me a vile name."

"What did he call you?" asked the judge.

"It's really too terrible to repeat. He ... he called me ... a ... two-bit whore!"

"That is bad," said the judge. "What did you hit him with?"

"A bag full of quarters!"

*   *   *

When the members of a great old Southern aristocratic family heard that their daughter Clarabelle, who lived up north, had become a lady of the evening, they were stunned and shocked.

"Imagine!" cried Uncle Stonewall in despair. "It's a disgrace. To think of one of our kinfolk having to work for a living!"

*   *   *

PIMP
Nookie Bookie

*   *   *

What do you get when you cross an elephant with a prostitute?

A 400-pound whore who will screw for peanuts.

101

Oscar walked into a fancy house and announced to the madam, "I have claustrophobia. I gotta have a girl out on the ledge."

"You wanna go up to the second floor and do it out on a window ledge?" she asked. "I might have someone who'll go along with your fetish."

Within five minutes a girl appeared, led Oscar upstairs, out to the ledge and they got going immediately. Just at that precious moment, they rolled off the ledge and landed on the sidewalk below—both unconscious, frozen in their love positions.

A drunk staggering up the street saw them lying there. He blinked his eyes, then walked up to the house and rapped on the door. "What do you want?" asked the madam.

"I thought you'd like to know," slobbered the drunk, "your sign fell down!"

A good-looking New York call girl flagged down a taxi on Eighth Avenue, hopped in, and directed the driver to a Long Island address. As the cab crossed over the 59th Street Bridge, the girl exclaimed, "Oh, my God! I forgot my purse!"

"Nuts!" said the driver. "How're you gonna pay me!"

"With this!" she answered, raising her skirt above her waist.

"You got anything smaller?" snapped the driver.

* * *

IDEAL JOB
Comparison shopper in a red-light district

* * *

Mabel's most liked of all the tramps.
Not so sexy, but she gives green stamps.

* * *

Hear about the guy who stood in front of a house of ill-repute on Halloween and kept yelling, "Trick or treat"?

* * *

HOOKER
A professional trampoline

True Menthol brings low tar and low nicotine to the 100mm smoker.

True Menthol 100's.

100's Regular and 100's Menthol.
12 mg. "tar", 0.7 mg. nicotine,
av. per cigarette, by FTC method.

True brings
low tar and low nicotine
to the 100mm smoker.
True 100's.

100's Regular and 100's Menthol:
12 mg. "tar", 0.7 mg. nicotine,
av. per cigarette, by FTC method.

© Lorillard 1975

Xaviera Hollander, the world's most famous hooker, has a great sense of humor. Here's a story she tells intimates:

It was late at night when the doorbell rang. The madam was awakened, slipped on a kimono, and opened the door. There stood a man with both arms and both legs in plaster casts.

"I want a woman!" he said.

"Look," she replied, "why don't you just go home. It's late and I'd like to get some sleep."

"I want a woman!" he repeated.

"Let's be realistic," she said. "What could you do with a woman in your condition?"

"Hey, lady," he replied. "I rang the bell, didn't I?"

* * *

Two Tennessee hillbillies met behind a still. "Howdy, Hiram," said the first.

"Howdy, Abner," replied the second. "Ain't seen you 'round these parts in a spell. Where ya been keepin' yerself?"

"Took a vacation," said Abner.

"Where'd ya go?"

"Nashville."

"Enjoy yerself?"

"Yep. Spent m'two weeks there livin' in one o' them brothels."

"That musta been mighty costly," said Hiram.

"Nope," said Abner. "Kinfolk."

Hollywood producers Jerry Cutler and Bucky Searles have a long list of great gags they entertain friends with. Here's one of them:

A joy girl fell in love with a wholesome Boston boy. He returned the affection, but he would not marry her because she was so stupid. She begged him to educate her and finally, he brought her to his friend, Walter, who was a professor at Harvard.

Walter taught the girl various subjects. After a year of intensive training, the wholesome Boston boy tested his call girl sweetheart and found, to his dismay, that she was just as stupid as ever.

MORAL: *You can lead a whore to Walter but you can't make her think.*

* * *

A sign in bold letters on the lawn in front of a church read:

IF TIRED OF SIN, COME IN

Under it, written in lipstick, was this message: *If not, call Ardmore 6-3621*

* * *

A notorious hooker named Hurst
In the pleasures of men is well versed.
  Reads a sign o'er the head
  Of her well-rumpled bed,
The Customer Always Comes First.

106

Then there was the professional lady who bought a bicycle and peddled it all over town.

A girl entered a drugstore and said to the attendant, "I bought a bottle of internal cleanser that you recommended and that stuff burned my insides."

"So what?" said the attendant. "We sell it. We don't make it."

"So I'm going to see a lawyer," she said.

And she did. She explained the circumstances and the attorney said, "All right, we'll sue for $5,000 and expenses. What business are you in?"

"I'm a prostitute," she replied.

"I'm sorry," he said, "but I can't handle your case."

She tried again and again, but she couldn't find a lawyer to take her case. Finally she ended up with a shyster attorney known for his disreputable clientele. "We'll sue for $10,000 and attorney's fees," he said. "What business are you in?"

"Well," she replied warily, "I'm a hooker."

"Even better," he crowed, rubbing his hands together. "We'll make that $20,000, and institute a second suit for arson.

"Arson?" she asked.

"Sure!" he smiled. "We'll claim they burned up your business."

* * *

The last of the sex maniacs . . .*

* turn over and try a virgin

The end of the virgins...*

* turn over and try a sex maniac

AS LONG AS THERE ARE VIRGINS, THERE'LL BE JOKES ABOUT THEM

In case you've forgotten, a virgin is:

* A girl who won't take in what a guy is taking out

* One who whispers sweet nothing-doings in your ear

* A female who hasn't yet met her maker

* An unlusted number

* A girl who ran all the way home because she was being chaste

* A 12-year-old Kentucky female who can run faster than all her brothers

Other Books by Larry Wilde

The Official Jewish/Irish Joke Book
The Official Polish/Italian Joke Book
Also, *The Great Comedians* (Citadel)

THE OFFICIAL VIRGINS JOKE BOOK

by Larry Wilde

Illustrations by Ron Wing

PINNACLE BOOKS • NEW YORK CITY

*For my beautiful wife, Maryruth, who
started out like the title of one side
of this book and wound up like the other!*

THE OFFICIAL VIRGINS/SEX MANIACS JOKE
BOOK

An original Pinnacle Books edition, published for the
first time anywhere.

ISBN: 0-523-00634-9

First printing, April 1975

Printed in the United States of America

PINNACLE BOOKS, INC.
275 Madison Avenue
New York, N. Y. 10016

ABOUT THE AUTHOR

Larry Wilde is a popular nightclub and television comedian who has performed at major entertainment spots with Debbie Reynolds, Ann-Margret, Wayne Newton, Vikki Carr, Pat Boone, and many others.

In addition, Mr. Wilde is frequently seen as an actor on TV in commercials, on talk shows, and on such series as "Adam 12," "Barnaby Jones," and "The Mary Tyler Moore Show."

Born in Jersey City, New Jersey, Larry served two years in the United States Marine Corps and has a bachelor's degree from the University of Miami, Florida. His writing credits include articles for professional journals as well as *Genesis*, *TV Guide*, *Penthouse*, *Coronet*, and other popular magazines.

Mr. Wilde is married and resides in Hollywood, where, between Las Vegas engagements, concert appearances, and university lectures, he conducts a class in comedy at UCLA.

CONTENTS

VIRGIN

Any 12-year-old Kentucky girl who can run faster than all her brothers!

THE AMATEURS

She: My mother told me to say "No" to everything.
He: Well, do you mind if I hold your hand?
She: No.
He: Do you mind if I put my arm around you?
She: No.
He: Honey, if you're on the level about this we're gonna have a great time tonight!

* * *

It's remarkable what some women can get by with and still keep their amateur standing.

* * *

A nightclub owner was interviewing a young waitress. After the usual questions, he ogled her and asked, "Are you a virgin?"

Realizing the job might hinge on her answer, she replied, "Yes, but I'm not a fanatic about it!"

1

The young beauty was confiding in her older and wiser sister about the events of the night before. "We went to a movie, then to a nice restaurant, and then I went up to his apartment for a few drinks. Did I do wrong?"

"Don't you remember?"

* * *

There were three sisters getting ready to go out for the evening. The eldest said, "Mother, I'm going out with Pete to eat!"

"All right, darling," said her mother, "be back early."

The second sister said, "I'm going out with Vance to dance!"

"All right!"

The youngest girl said, "I'm going out with Chuck!"

"Oh, no you're not! You're staying right here!"

* * *

RINGSIDE RAG

She Was Only the Prizefighter's Daughter, but She Knew How to Act in a Clinch.

* * *

"Do you know the difference between a popular girl and an unpopular one?"

"Yes and no."

2

Then there was the girl who ran all the way home one night because she was being chaste.

* * *

"What was that you said, Phillip?" she asked as she loosened her shoulder straps.

"Say it again, dear." She let her dress slide to the floor.

"I can hardly believe it!" She stepped out of her shoes, drew up a chair, and slowly peeled off her panty hose.

"Promise me you won't tell a soul," she implored, her voice quivering with excitement. She wiggled slightly and her sheer underthings slipped and fell in a heap of perfumed ruffles at her feet.

"All right, Phillip—good night!"

And she hung up.

* * *

THE AMOROUS AMATEUR

The moon was yellow;
The lane was bright.
She turned to me
In the summer night.
And with every glance
She gave a hint
That what she craved
Was real romance.
I stammered, stuttered
And time went by.
The moon was yellow
...And so was I!

3

On a Hollywood movie lot the script girl approached the young starlet. "In this first reel you're supposed to look virginal."

"What do you think I am," replied the ingenue, "a character actress!"

* * *

MISTAKE
Something a virgin and a parachute jumper can only make once

* * *

Girl: There's one thing I want to tell you before you go any *further.*
Boy: What's that?
Girl: Don't go any *further!*

* * *

Emeralds and rubies, diamonds and pearls
And a yacht on the bounding main
Will never replace true love, sweet girls,
But, oh, how it eases the pain.

* * *

Babette flounced out of the house in a hurry and as she reached the sidewalk, her mother called, "Have a good time at the dance tonight, dear, and be a good girl!"

"Mother, make up your mind!"

KLEPTOMANIAC
A snatch thief. Greatly feared by virgins.

* * *

My parents taught me not to smoke.
    I don't.
Nor to listen to a dirty joke. I don't.
They made it clear I must not wink at
    handsome boys,
Nor even think about intoxicating drink.
    I don't.
To sow my wild oats they say is wrong.
    I don't.
My girl friends chase men, drink wine.
    I don't.
I don't kiss boys, not a single one.
I don't even know how it's done.
You'd think that I wouldn't have much fun.
Well, you're right. I *don't!*

* * *

Mother: Why do you go riding with
            strange men?
Daughter: Well, they don't act strange un-
            til I go out riding with them.

* * *

"Do you know what virgins eat for
breakfast?" asked Hector in a seductive
tone.

"No," replied Pearl coyly. "What?"

"Hmmm," said Hector, "just as I
thought."

"I always resist whenever fellows try to kiss me on dates because I remember what my mother taught me."

"Then I imagine you don't have too much fun on dates, do you?"

"Of course I do. I always go out with guys who are stronger than I am."

* * *

Cab driver: Did someone tell me to stop?
Man: Keep going stupid! She wasn't talking to you!

* * *

"Some moon out tonight, isn't it, Maryjane?"

"Oh, yes."

"Some beautiful starry sky, isn't it, Maryjane?"

"Oh, yes."

"Some dew on the grass, Maryjane."

"Yeah, but I don't!"

* * *

VIRGIN MONKEY

A monkey that doesn't allow another monkey to monkey around with her monkey

When loyalty questionnaires had to be filled out by government employees all over the country, a rugged individualist in San Francisco put down some information that gave the examiners something to think about.

In the space devoted to her foreign activities, this young lady wrote:

"Before World War II, I spent a year in Germany. Does this make me a Nazi? I also spent one year in Russia. Does this make me a Communist? I also own a piece of property in the Virgin Islands."

* * *

He (trying to make conversation): Honey, there's the ol' sun rising for the first time this year!

She (sleepily): Well, as you told me last night, there always has to be a first time.

* * *

WISDOM
Knowing What to Do

SKILL
Knowing How to Do It

VIRTUE
Not Doing It

7

She: Get out of my apartment. I never want to see you again. Go this instant!

He: I have one last request to make before I leave forever.

She (*sweetly*): Yes, what is it?

He: Get off my lap!

* * *

VIRGIN

A girl who won't take in what a fellow is taking out

* * *

After two hours of battling in a parked convertible, Betty managed to protest to her date, "Do you know what good clean fun is?"

"No," he answered, "what good is it?"

* * *

The couple were hugging and kissing with the lights off. "What are you thinking about?" she whispered.

"The same thing you are!" he replied hotly.

"Then I'll race you to the refrigerator," she shouted.

* * *

Nine farmer's daughters—that's right, nine—forced a traveling salesman into

promising to make love to each of them. They did it by threatening to wake their sleeping father who had a shotgun ready at his side.

When it got to be her turn, the fifth daughter threatened the salesman, who by now was exhausted. "Come on now," she said, "or I'll tell papa!"

"Then you better tell your father," he whimpered. "I'd rather be shot than screwed to death!"

*　*　*

This is a tale of a traveling sales*woman*. She was in bed with the farmer's son. "How about trading sides with me?" she suggested. "You roll over me and I'll roll over you, and we'll get more comfortable."

They did this several times without much result. "You know," said the woman, "I don't think you know what I really want."

"The hell I don't!" replied the farmer's son, "you want the whole damn bed, but you ain't goin' to get it!"

*　*　*

Brad and Jenny, who lived on neighboring farms, were watching a bull servicing a cow. The boy began to get excited and said to the farmer's daughter, "Believe me, I'd sure like to be doing what that bull is doing!"

"Why don't you?" asked Jenny. "It's your cow!"

9

Richard O. Linke, the prominent show business personal manager, gets screams from TV execs with this one:

A beautiful girl appeared at the gates of heaven and wanted to be admitted. Saint Peter asked her the routine question: "Are you a virgin?"

"Of course," she replied.

To make sure, Saint Peter instructed an angel doctor to examine the girl. When he had finished, the M.D. reported, "I think we can let her in, but I must report that there were seven slight dents in her maidenhead."

Saint Peter decided he couldn't deny her admittance for such a trifle, so he sent her along to the registration desk. "Your name?" asked the clerk.

"Snow White," she answered.

My name is Snow White!

11

VIRGIN WOOL

Wool from a sheep that could outrun the farmer

* * *

A Kansas farmhand visiting Chicago was taken by a taxi driver to a house of ill repute. The farmer was struck by the politeness of the girl who called her mother "Madam."

In the morning, he dressed carefully and was about to leave. "What about some money?" asked the girl.

"No, thanks, M'am!" said the hick. "You've been more than kind already!"

* * *

Farmer Moore had mortgaged the farm to give his daughter a college education. Now driving home from the station after meeting her at the train, he was greatly disturbed when she announced, "I have a confession to make, Paw. I ain't a virgin no more."

"After all the sacrifices your Maw and I made to give you a good education," sighed the old man sadly, "you still say 'ain't'!"

* * *

"Did he get fresh?"

"I'll say he did. I had to slap him three times before I gave in."

The young secretary complained to the police. "This guy went up to my apartment with me," she said, "threw me on the bed, tore off all my clothes, and then ran off with my purse!"

"Did you scream?" asked one of the officers.

"Of course not," she replied. "How did I know he was going to rob me!"

*　　*　　*

"Albert Rogers came over to my house last night, and as he was leaving he asked me to wear his college ring. But I told him I couldn't wear it until I knew him better."

"But you're wearing it now!"

"Well, he didn't leave right then!"

*　　*　　*

SLIDING ZIPPER
The last thing a girl hears as a virgin

*　　*　　*

Professor Jackson was winding up his welcoming speech to the incoming freshmen at an all-boys school. "And remember," he said, "you can't always be first. Look at George Washington, the father of our country. He was first in war, first in peace, first in the hearts of his countrymen, and still he married a widow!"

13

When a college girl's sofa is a beehive of activity, it's a sure sign a little honey is being made.

* * *

Barbara got a job with an advertising agency distributing little boxes of candy to the public. When she finished her day's work, she met an old friend. "How are you?" asked Barbara. "I heard you were getting married next month!"

"That's right," said the friend. "What are you doing now?"

"Nothing much," said Barbara. "Just giving away free samples."

* * *

They were saying goodnight after their first date. "Thanks for the hug and the kiss."

"Don't mention it. The pressure was all mine."

* * *

I draw the line at kissing,
She said in accents fine.
But he was a football hero
And of course he crossed the line.

* * *

How about the co-ed who went to the big homecoming game and came home with a bad case of athlete's fetus?

14

At the homecoming dance the beauty queen was surrounded by admirers. She looked simply ravishing so it took a great deal of courage for a timid sophomore to approach her. "May I have the next dance?"

"I'm sorry," she said with an amused smile, "but I never dance with children."

"Pardon me," he replied. "I didn't know about your condition!"

* * *

College professor: Who made you, little girl?

Freshman co-ed: Originally or lately?

* * *

SATURDAY NIGHT IN A COLLEGE TOWN

That's the night the girls sow their wild oats. Then Sunday morning they pray for a crop failure.

* * *

CATHOLIC COLLEGE GIRL'S PRAYER

Oh, Blessed Virgin, we believe
That thou without sin didst conceive.
Teach us, then, how thus believing
We can sin without conceiving.

15

The Dean of Women at an all-girls college ended her passionate morals and anti-sex lecture to the incoming freshmen: "And so girls, wherever you go, remember you represent Norfolk. No smoking in the streets, no shorts in the classroom, no unseemly conversation on the stairs. And above all, when the men bother you, ask yourselves, 'Is an hour of pleasure worth a lifetime of disgrace?' Now are there any questions?"

"Yeah!" asked a blonde in the back row. "How do you make it last an hour?"

* * *

At a slumber party the co-eds got to talking about the girls they knew who put out.

"What does 'put out' mean?" asked one inexperienced brunette.

"Well, honey," explained a senior, "a girl who 'puts out' is one who offers the guy something to put it in!"

* * *

"Did Jack ever propose to you?"
"Yeah. Everything but marriage!"

* * *

Two college boys were discussing girls —on a higher plane.

"I know a girl who goes to bed every night at eight. She doesn't smoke, drink, or swear and she never thinks of sex."

"That's marvelous."

"I don't know. She'll be five years old tomorrow."

* * *

NICE GIRL
One who whispers sweet nothing-doings in your ear

* * *

There was a young co-ed at Kent
Who said that she knew what it meant
   When men asked her to dine,
   Gave her cocktails and wine,
She knew what it meant . . . but she went.

* * *

Calling on an attractive co-ed, the theology professor asked, "Who was the first man?"

"If it's all the same to you, sir," replied the embarrassed girl, "I'd rather not tell."

* * *

HEN PARTY
A bunch of birds clucking about who is laying whom

Mother: Why did it take you so long to say goodnight to your date?

Daughter: But mother, if a fellow takes you to the movies, the least you can do is give him a kiss.

Mother: But I thought he was taking you to an expensive nightclub.

Daughter: He did.

* * *

After repeatedly warding off her date's amorous advances during the evening, the pretty young stenographer decided to put her foot down.

"Look," she snapped, "this is positively the last time I'm going to tell you 'no.' "

"Great!" exclaimed her date. "Now we can start making some progress."

* * *

Backstage of the Broadway musical, two chorus cuties were chatting. "You know that big Texan that asked me to have a drink with him after the show?" asked one of the girls of her friend.

"Yeah?"

"Well, he gave me a gorgeous diamond."

"Did it cut glass?"

"No, but it certainly cut the ice!"

18

Nancy Stoudt, executive secretary par excellence, overheard this conversation in the bridal section of a department store:

"Have you been married before?" asked the salesclerk of the sweet young bride-to-be.

"Why no," she replied. "Why do you ask?"

"Well, when a girl has been previously married, it is customary to wear lavender rather than white."

"Oh. Then let's see what you have in white with a lavender trim."

* * *

She: Go out with you? Well, will you promise not to fool around?

He: Yes, yes. I'll promise.

She: Then I'm going out with Harry. He wouldn't promise.

* * *

Two young Hollywood hopefuls were sitting at Schwab's counter. "I sat in that casting director's office all day and I never got to see him," said the first gal.

"Did you keep your fingers crossed?" asked her friend.

"I was too busy keeping my legs crossed."

Barney had been shipwrecked on a desert island for ten years. One day a beautiful naked woman was washed ashore on a beer barrel and Barney revived her.

"Now that you've been so good to me," she said, "I'm going to give you something you haven't had for ten years."

"You mean," he exclaimed, "there's some beer in that barrel?"

21

Two showgirls were talking in the dressing room. "When that millionaire kissed me," said the first gal, "I immediately brought action against him."

"What kind of action?" asked her friend.

"Swaying from side to side!"

* * *

At a famous Las Vegas hotel, the director of entertainment walked into a rehearsal and asked the choreographer what was going on. "Those eight girls are doing the Dance of the Virgins!" he explained.

"Sure tough on seven of them to have to do it from memory!" answered the entertainment director.

* * *

CASANOVA'S CONSENSUS

Virgins are like new shoes—the more you wear them, the better they fit.

* * *

Sometimes a girl can't remember a man's face, but his hands are certainly familiar.

Dr. Bob Abeloff, the eminent Beverly Hills dentist, tells this favorite to patients:

"How about joining me for a cozy weekend in a quiet Palm Springs motel?" he whispered in the ear of a curvaceous cutie.

"I'm afraid," she responded, "that my awareness of your proclivities in the esoteric aspects of sexual behavior precludes you from such erotic confrontation."

"I don't get it!" he said.

"Exactly," she said with a smile.

* * *

He: I had a dream about you last night.
She: Did you?
He: No, you wouldn't let me.

* * *

VIRGIN SURGEON
Drugstore slang for a cherry Dr. Pepper

* * *

Two girls absentmindedly undressed in front of an open hotel window. One caught a bad cold, the other a rich bachelor.

Los Angeles stockbroker, Diane Lombardo, tells about the Californian who just got back from a trip to France.

"It was the darndest trip," he told a friend. "I picked up this little girl in Paris, drew a picture of a taxi, and sure enough she took me for a drive along the Seine.

"Then I drew a picture of a table and chair and we went to this restaurant. After some wine and a great meal, she draws a picture of a four-poster bed!"

"That's great!" exclaimed his friend.

"Yeah," said the Californian, "but I still can't figure out how the hell she knew I was in the furniture business!"

*   *   *

RELUCTANT VIRGIN
One who doesn't want to be one

*   *   *

He: How's about it, honey?
She: (*No answer*)
He: I said, how's about it?
She: (*No answer*)
He: Whatsamatta, ya deaf?
She: Whatsamatta, ya paralyzed?

*   *   *

"How does a deserving girl get herself a mink?"

"The same way minks do."

24

The bishop and his wife were sitting in a box in the college auditorium where graduation exercises were being held. The gowns worn by the braless young ladies were décolleté. Eeach time a co-ed bowed after receiving her sheepskin the bishop's wife let out a gasp.

"Honestly, Henry!" she exclaimed. "Did you ever see anything like it in your life?"

"No, dear," he replied gravely. "Not since I was weaned."

* * *

"My mother always told me to be good," said the demure, disheveled young damsel as she pulled up the sheets. "Was I?"

* * *

Jeanette Mintz, the beautiful Beverly Hills socialite, provides this provocative conundrum:

What's the difference between a good girl and a bad girl?

A good girl wakes up and says, "Good morning, Lord!"

A bad girl wakes up and says, "Good Lord, morning!"

* * *

MAIDEN
A girl who hasn't yet met her maker

25

Rube Auerbach, dynamic director of the Jersey Truck Center, heard this dilly from one of the drivers:

A girl driving through the desert ran out of gas. An Indian gave her a ride, sitting behind him on his pony. Every few minutes as they rode he let out a wild whooping yell that echoed across the desert. Finally, he deposited her at a gas station and went off with a last "Yah-hoo!"

"What were you doing?" asked the station owner, "to make that injun do all that hollerin'?"

"Nothing!" said the girl. "I just sat behind him with my arms around his sides, holding on to his saddle horn."

"Miss," said the man, "Indians ride bareback!"

26

Miss, Indians ride bareback!

27

He: Oh, Oh! I think I heard something break.

She: Never mind. That was just my promise to mother.

* * *

Dick approached a delicious tidbit sitting at the bar of a singles lounge. She wore a plaid skirt and a low-cut, V-neck sweater. "Hi," said Dick, undressing her mentally.

"Hello, handsome!"

His eyes focused on her sweater and the curves it *almost* covered. "What's the *V* stand for?" he asked, "Veronica?"

"Uh uh. Virgin."

"What?" he exclaimed. "You're a virgin?"

"No," she winked. "It's last year's sweater."

* * *

COMPLAINT TO VIRGINITY
A big issue
Over a little tissue

* * *

She: Last night I was kissed sixty times in one hour.

He: By the clock?

She: No, by the television set.

28

Ralph's amibition was to marry a virgin, so he picked a gal right out of convent school. In the lobby of the hotel where they were going to spend their wedding night, the bride was amazed by the beautiful unaccompanied women floating about.

"Who are they?" asked the girl.

"Those are prostitutes!" replied her husband.

"What's that?" asked the former convent student.

"A prostitute," explained Ralph, "is a woman that will sleep with any man that gives her fifty or a hundred dollars!"

"Gee," said the girl, "the priests only gave us an apple!"

*   *   *

"The artist I pose for is a painter, a sculptor, and a wood engraver."

"Yes, but I imagine he does one thing better than any of the others."

"Sure he does, but you can't pay the rent with that!"

*   *   *

SEMI-VIRGIN
*A girl who tried it once
and didn't like it*

Steve Saunders, the guiding genius of *Genesis* magazine, came up with this gem:

New photocopying machines were installed in the oil company's exploration office and placed in the care of Rosemary, one of the more shapely secretaries. The office remained open 24 hours each day because of a research staff working on three shifts.

It soon developed that the research boys on the night shift were using the new duplicating machines and leaving a big mess for Rosemary to clean up the next day.

She complained several times to the office manager who finally posted this sign on the door of her office:

NOTICE
No one shall use Rosemary's reproduction equipment without express permission of the office manager.

* * *

IMPATIENT VIRGIN
The only hunter who uses herself as bait

* * *

A policeman stumbled on a young couple making love in a graveyard and

dragged them into night court. "What were you doing in a graveyard at midnight?" asked the judge.

"Nothing wrong, your honor," replied the boy. "We were just burying the old stiff."

"And how about you?" the judge asked the girl.

"I was the undertaker," she responded.

"You idiot!" yelled the judge at the policeman. "I fine *you* twenty-five dollars for disturbing the peace!"

* * *

"I'm awfully sorry, Miss," said the store clerk, "but this twenty-dollar bill is counterfeit."

"Damn it!" she exclaimed. "I've been seduced!"

* * *

She: How dare you kiss me like that?
He: Sorry, it was just a slip of the tongue.

* * *

METALLURGIST

*A man who can take one look at
a platinum blonde and tell whether she
is virgin metal or common ore*

Frank Vernon, jovial jeweler by trade and master raconteur by acclamation, regales Lakeside Country Club laddies with this lulu:

Marge lived in a one-room flat with her sister. Her new boyfriend, Brick, shared a small apartment with an aunt. After dating several weeks, Marge and Brick had been unable to find a spot where they could be alone.

Walking back to Marge's place one night, the couple passed a cemetery. "No one would bother us in there," suggested Brick. Marge agreed.

The next morning, Marge woke up with a terrible ache in her neck. "Take a look at my neck, sis," she asked. "I've got an awful pain!"

The sister looked closely. "There's nothing wrong with your neck, Marge," she said. "But your back died in 1869."

* * *

Blessed are the pure,
For they shall inhibit the earth!

* * *

THE UNTOUCHABLES

Here lie the bones of Martha Jones.
For her Hell has no terrors.
Born a virgin—died a virgin,
No hits—no runs—no errors!

*   *   *

OLD MAID
One who has given up all hope of giving in

*   *   *

A spinster told the young lawyer who was making out her will that she had $2,000. Half was to go for her burial expenses and the other half to him if he would spend the night with her so she would not have to die a virgin.

Three days later, when the lawyer had not come home, his wife rushed over to the old maid's house. "Is my husband here?" she demanded.

"Yes, dearie! I've decided to let the *town* bury me!"

INSCRIPTION ON AN OLD MAID'S TOMBSTONE

Who said you can't take it with you?.

* * *

"They tell me your spinster aunt died quite happily."

"Yes. Somebody told her marriages are made in heaven."

* * *

Hettie Smith, aged 70, died a spinster. She left the following instructions in her will: "I don't want anybody to put the word 'Miss' on my tombstone. I haven't missed as much as some people think."

* * *

UNATTACHED LADY'S BEDTIME PRAYER

Now I lay me down to sleep.
I wish I had a man to keep.
If there's a man beneath my bed.
I hope he heard each word I said.

* * *

Aunt Tillie (praying): "Oh, Lord, I ask nothing for myself, but would you please send my dear mother a son-in-law!"

"And Aunt Ethel never married?"

"She was two-thirds married once. She was there and the preacher was there; but the man didn't show up!"

* * *

Visiting curate: I really wish you could see the altar of our church.
Spinster: Lead me to it.

* * *

Aunt Sophie was given a parrot by her nephew who was in the navy. It was a beautiful bird but unfortunately it used the foulest language. She decided to take up her problem with her pastor.

"I have a parrot, too," said the clergyman. "I call her Clementine. She's very devout. Prays constantly. We'll bring the two birds together, put them in one cage, and before you know it, a little of Clementine's religion will rub off on your parrot."

The next day the meeting was arranged and the parrots gave each other the once-over from opposite corners of the cage.

Suddenly, Aunt Sophie's bird screeched, "How about it, gorgeous?"

The pastor's parrot looked startled for a moment, and then said, "Sure, big boy! What the hell do you think I've been *praying* for?"

An elderly spinster sniffed when anyone suggested that it was too bad she did not have a husband.

"I have a dog that growls, a parrot that swears, a fireplace that smokes, and a cat that stays out all night. Why should I want a husband?"

* * *

EPITAPH ON AN OLD MAID'S TOMBSTONE
Returned ... unopened

* * *

Many an old maid feels the world owes her a loving.

* * *

Myrtle and Lucille were discussing men. "What do you desire most in a husband," asked Myrtle, "brains, wealth, or appearance?"

"Appearance," snapped Lucille, "and the sooner the better!"

* * *

Lady: Officer, that man on the corner is annoying me.
Policeman: I saw the whole thing, and that man wasn't even looking at you.
Lady: Well, isn't that annoying?

"Connie swears she's never slept with a man, petted, or even kissed."

"Well, wouldn't you swear, too!"

*   *   *

Steve Dweck, Debbie Reynolds' marvelous nightclub musical director, passed this one along:

Evangeline was a terribly unattractive woman. She had protruding teeth, a large nose, and sixty pounds of extra weight. She was trying to sleep on the lower berth of a train, but unfortunately, she couldn't because of the man snoring in the upper berth.

She kept rapping on the metal partition but each time the man woke up, he fell back asleep and began snoring again.

Finally, Evangeline banged on the metal furiously. "It's no use, lady!" grumbled the man above. "I saw you get on!"

*   *   *

Hettie and Lottie were given the address of a male brothel by an understanding physician. On their way, they passed a barber shop where the owner was burning hair behind the store.

The spinsters whiffed the air and then looked at each other. "Say," said Hettie, "do you think we're walking too fast?"

The bus was crowded and the elderly spinster felt her small purse being snatched from her hand. She turned quickly and thought she saw a suspicious-looking character slip it into his pocket. Indignantly, she jabbed her hand into his pocket, gasped, and then fainted.

"Say," said a man who had seen the whole incident, "what have you got in your pocket?"

"Who's got pockets?" answered the character, shrugging his shoulders.

* * *

Comedian Charlie Dornan swears this happened at the Brockton, Massachusetts, post office:

A spinster saw a handsome fellow's picture in a "Wanted" poster and offered $100 more than the FBI.

* * *

MAIDEN AUNT

An old gal who never had sense enough to holler "Uncle!"

* * *

Burglar: Don't be scared, old lady, all I want is your money.

Old maid: Go away. You're just like all the other men.

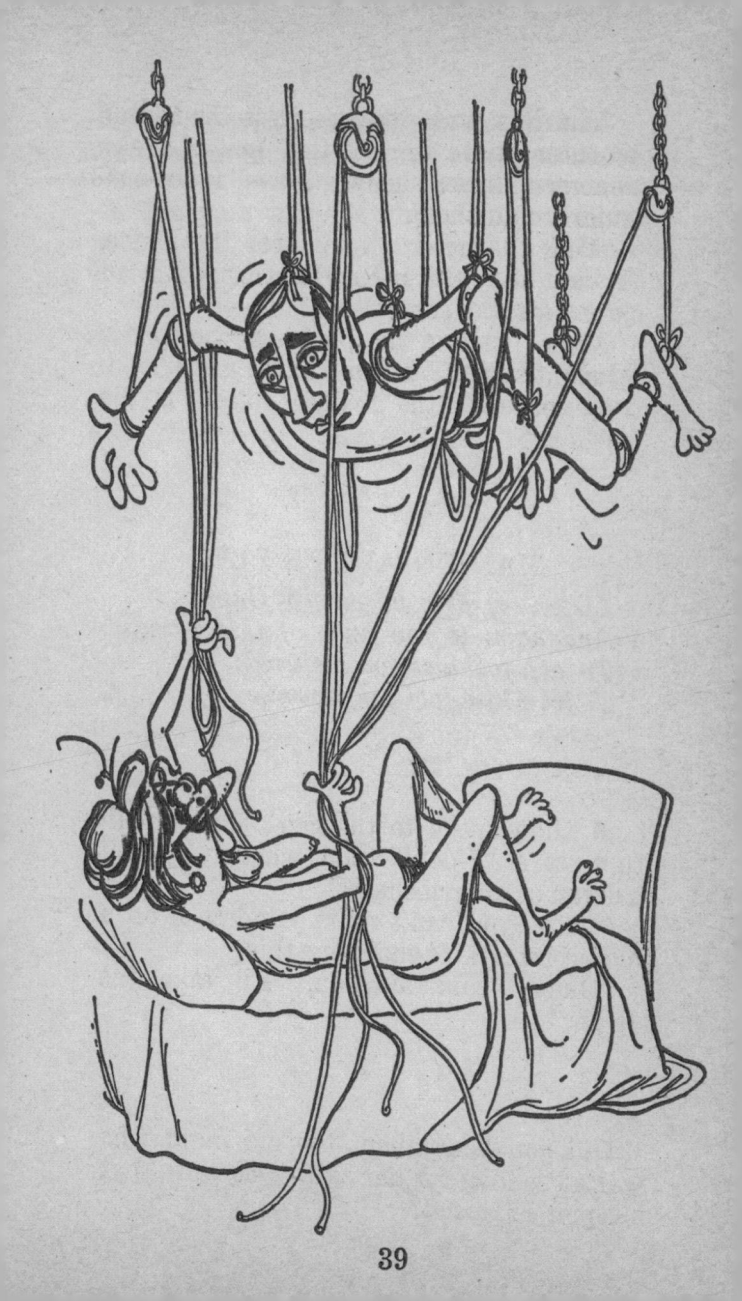

Johnny Leong, the peerless fruit and produce purveyor at the Los Angeles Farmers Market, gets guffaws from customers on this one:

"Police?" cried a voice over the phone. "I want to report a burglar trapped in an old maid's bedroom!"

After getting the address the police sergeant said, "Who am I talking to?"

"This," said the frantic voice, "is the burglar."

* * *

MAIDEN AUNT'S PLEA

Listen my girls, be wary of Cupid
And hark to the lines of this verse.
To let a fool kiss you is stupid;
To let a kiss fool you is worse.

* * *

Matilda spoke to the clerk in a furniture store. "I don't know whether I want a divan or an armchair."

"Lady, you can't make a mistake on a nice, comfortable chair like this."

"Okay," said Matilda, "I'll take the divan."

* * *

Did you hear about the old maid who waited so long for her ship to come in that her pier collapsed?

In a supermarket, a very straight-laced, dignified female of the old school walked up to a girl who was smoking. "I just think it's terrible the way young girls smoke nowadays," she said, "I'd rather be raped by a dozen men than smoke a cigarette!"

"Who the hell wouldn't!" snapped the modern miss.

* * *

Then there were the two old maids who were on a drunk and he couldn't get them off.

* * *

Old maid (calling the fire department): A man is trying to get into my room.
Voice: You don't want the fire department—what you want is the police department.
Old maid: I don't want the police. I want the fire department! A man is trying to get into my room, and I'm on the second floor and he needs a ladder.

* * *

Virginia had been living alone for many years, and now she was determined to do something about it. She rang the fire alarm and twenty firemen responded. When they arrived, Virginia told them, "There's no fire, so nineteen of you can go back."

A spinster was attending a wrestling match. Suddenly one of the wrestlers was thrown in her lap, but she refused to give him up, yelling, "Finders keepers!"

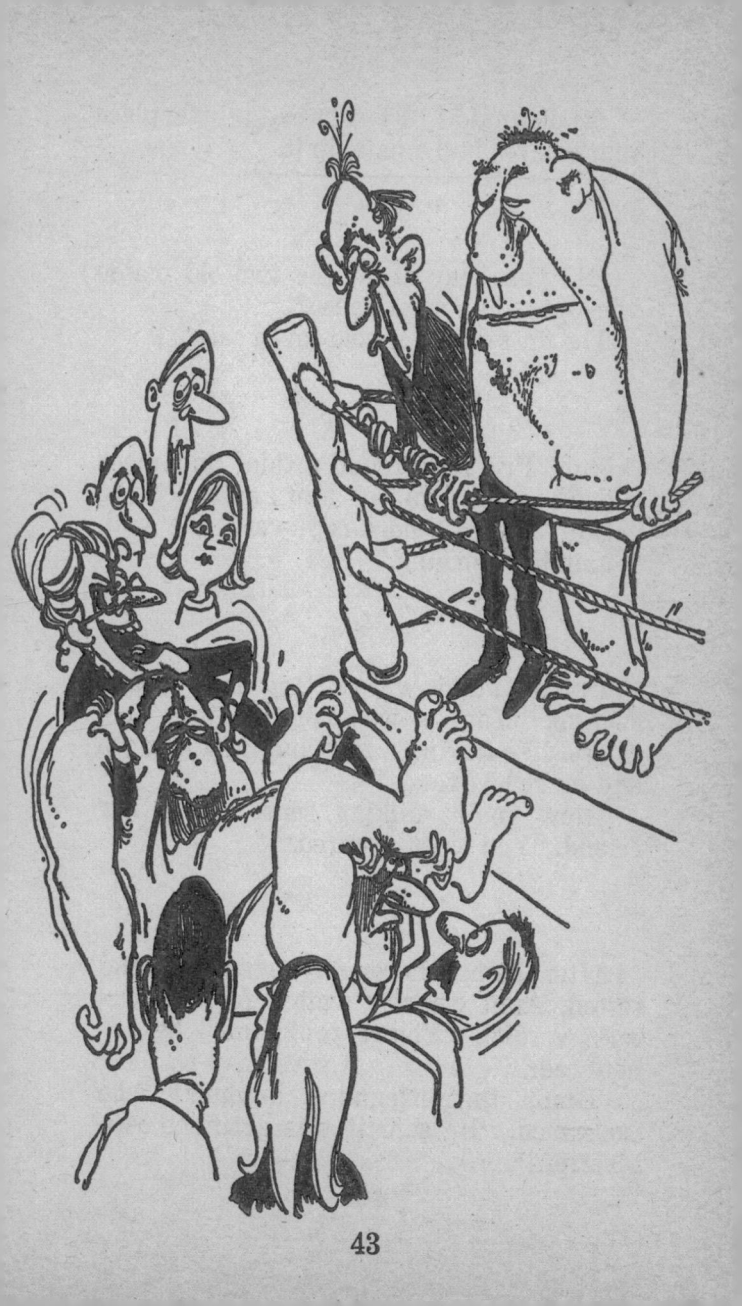

An old maid in Florida had a little place that's never had a palm in it.

* * *

Did you hear about the two old maids who opened up a cat house?
The first day they sold seven cats.

* * *

Aunt Prudence found a thief under her bed. She held a gun on him and called the police. "Please send a cop over," she said, "... in the morning."

* * *

Two old maids were sitting in an insane asylum. "You know," said the first one, "I feel like having a man hug and kiss me and make love to me!"
"Now you're talking sense," said her friend. "You must be cured."

* * *

After being thoroughly examined and tested, Aunt Charity waited for the doctor's verdict. "You're pregnant!" he announced.
"Damn that lifeguard, anyhow!" she exclaimed. "He said it was artificial respiration!"

44

One day Miss Tilly saw her big tom cat corner a cockroach in the kitchen. He was about to kill the bug when it addressed Miss Tilly. "Have your cat spare my life and I'll grant you three wishes."

"A million dollars?" asked the spinster.

"Granted!" said the roach, producing the money. "I want to be young and beautiful!"

"You got it!" And she was.

"Now," said Tilly, "turn my tom cat into a tall, handsome prince lying next to me in bed!" It was done.

"I'm so happy!" she exclaimed.

"I'm glad," said the Prince beside her. "But aren't you sorry now you had me fixed?"

* * *

Adelaide and Genevieve were leaving the museum of art. "For such a large statue of Hercules," said Adelaide, "didn't he have awfully small organs?"

"Yes," said Genevieve, "and so *cold*, too."

* * *

OLD MAID
A girl whose father never owned a shotgun

Did you hear about the mean ventriloquist who went around throwing his voice under the beds of old maids?

*　　*　　*

NEWS FLASH
Old maids can now buy cellophane mattresses, so they don't have to jump out of bed to see who's underneath.

*　　*　　*

Irene: Auntie, were you ever in a predicament?
Maiden aunt: No, dearie. But Heaven knows, I tried!

*　　*　　*

Margaret and Valerie met at the market. "I just read where Mrs. Green had her husband cremated!" said Margaret.

"Isn't that always the way?" announced Valerie. "Some of us can't get one, and others have husbands to burn!"

*　　*　　*

SPINSTER
An Unlusted Number

"Yvonne could have married anybody she pleased."

"Then why is she still single?"

"She never pleased anybody."

*   *   *

They were on a sleigh ride. If Annabelle played her cards right, her days of being an old maid would soon be over. She heaved a deep sigh for the benefit of the eligible young man beside her.

"What's the matter, Miss Annabelle?" he asked.

She managed an artistic catch in her throat. "Nobody loves me and my hands are cold."

"Now don't you fret," he comforted her. "God loves you and you can sit on your hands."

*   *   *

"Is it true, Miss Crenshaw, that you are going to be married soon?"

"Well, no it isn't. But I am very grateful for the rumor."

*   *   *

What do you call a woman who's afraid of flies?

An old maid.

Manny Harmon, the society orchestra leader for America's VIP functions, came up with this doozy:

A Las Vegas cowboy had lost heavily at the crap table and decided to rob someone to cover his losses. Standing on a darkened street corner, he waited for a victim. In a few minutes an old maid came walking by.

"Don't move!" said the Vegas cowpoke. "This is a stickup!"

"What do you want?" asked the spinster.

"I want your money!" demanded the cowboy.

"I haven't got any," said the woman.

"I'll see for myself," declared the cowboy, and began searching her.

First he looked in her purse but found nothing. Then he searched her bra and it too was empty. He then ran his hands up her legs, figuring she might have some cash hidden inside her stockings. Not finding any money there, he started to leave but the old maid pulled him back.

"Don't stop searching me now," she cried. "I'll write you a check!"

48

Don't stop now. I'll write you a check!

Jeraldine Saunders, Glendale's gorgeous astrologer and author, saves this one for when the stars are just right:

Rupert loved Miss Holly who was an old maid. But he was painfully shy and could never work up the courage to pop the question. At last he decided to test his fate and did it by telephone.

"Miss Holly?" he asked, when she answered the first ring.

"This is she speaking!"

"Will you, ah, er, marry me?" Rupert stammered.

"Why, of course," replied Holly promptly. "Who is this, please?"

* * *

"*Cats* my dear," exclaimed the spinster. "I hate the very sight of them. I had a sweet little canary and some cat got that. I had a perfect parrot, and some cat got that. I had an adorable *fiance*, and . . . oh, don't mention cats to me!"

* * *

Aunt Lulu dreamed that she was married. But when she woke up, she found that there wasn't anything in it.

Once upon a time there was a little girl who had many boyfriends. They each asked her, "Do you love me?" She answered "yes" to each of them. This went on for many years, but she died an old maid anyway.

MORAL: *Don't love everybody.*
Specialize!

* * *

Vera had just returned from spending a weekend at a hotel in the city. She and her friend Sarah were talking about it. "I bet that man was embarrassed when you caught him looking over the transom," said Sarah.

"Gosh, yes," replied Vera. "I thought he'd never get over it."

* * *

Two elderly spinsters bought a farm and went to see a farmer about stocking it with chickens. "We want 300 chickens and 300 roosters," said the older one.

"M'am," said the farmer, "for 300 chickens all you need is thirty roosters."

"No," said the younger woman. "We want 300 chickens and 300 roosters. We know what it means to be lonesome!"

Adam and Rodney Williams were twins. Adam was married. Rodney owned a dilapidated rowboat. Strangely enough, on the day that Adam's wife died, Rodney's rowboat sank.

The next day, Aunt Marjorie mistook Rodney for the brother whose wife had just died. "Oh, Mr. Williams," she said kindly, "I'm so sorry to hear of your loss!"

"I'm not a bit sorry for she was a rotten old thing from the start," said Rodney. "Her bottom was all chewed up, she smelled of fish, and the first time I used her, she made water faster than anything I ever saw. It finally got so I couldn't handle her.

"Then one day, some guy used her and she leaked like the dickens. But the thing that finished her was one day I rented her to some guys looking for a good time. I explained to them what she was like, but they said they'd take a chance with her anyway. Well, the damn fools tried to use her all at one time and that was too much for her for she cracked right up the middle."

Aunt Marjorie fainted dead away.

*　　*　　*

Martha and Prudence were sitting in the hotel lounge. "If I have another drink," said Martha, "I'll begin to feel it!"

"If *I* have another drink," said Prudence, "I won't care who feels it."

ECSTASY

*The feeling you feel when you feel you
are going to feel a feeling you never
felt before*

*   *   *

Then there was the old maid who sued
a Miami Beach hotel for cruelty. It seems
they gave her a room between two honey-
mooning couples.

*   *   *

A schoolteacher in her middle forties
allowed herself to be seduced for the first
time by the principal. She leaped out of
bed and stood sobbing by the window be-
rating herself.

"Oh, how can I get up in front of those
innocent children tomorrow," she cried,
"and pretend to be worthy of teaching
them, when I've been so sinful so often."

"Often?" said the principal. "I thought
this was the first time."

"Well, you're going to do it again,
aren't you?"

*   *   *

A young girl and her maiden aunt were
captured by enemy soldiers who prepared
to rape them.

"Oh, please don't!" pleaded the girl.

"Be quiet, honey," said the aunt.
"These soldiers have their orders. War is
war!"

Abigail and Grace were buying bananas. They were ten cents each, or three for a quarter. "Oh, well," said Abigail, "we can always *eat* the extra one!"

* * *

Jack Ginsberg, the Chicago golfer-pharmacist, saves this one for special friends:

Two maiden sisters owned a drugstore. One day, a young fellow walked in. "I'd like to talk to a male clerk," he said to one of the spinsters behind the counter.

"Don't be shy," said the woman. "We've been told just about everything."

"I need some sort of pill to calm me down," said the customer. "I have a terrible habit. Every time I see a girl, I wanna grab her and make love to her. What can you give me?"

"Just a minute," replied the old maid. "I'll discuss it with my sister."

She was back in less than two minutes. "Well?" said the man.

"My sister and I decided," said the old maid, "the best we could give you is $10,000 and the store."

* * *

THE NEWLYWEDS

Just married Doug and Ruth left the reception in a cab to spend the first night of their honeymoon in an out-of-the-way motel. The cab driver wasn't too sure how to get there. Doug and Ruth, however, couldn't wait and so they began making love in the back seat.

Seeing a fork in the road ahead, the driver said, "I take the next turn, right?"

"No," said the groom, "this one's all mine!"

* * *

UPS AND DOWNS
What life is full of. If you don't believe it, ask the new bride.

* * *

Groom: Bet you can't be undressed by the time I spell B-R-I-D-E.
Bride: Bet YOU can't be undressed by the time I spell G-R-O-O—— MMMMM....

Alfred and Mabel were going to elope. Alfred climbed the ladder and rapped on Mabel's windowpane. She opened the window softly.

"Are you ready?" he asked.

"Shh! Not so loud!" whispered Mabel. "I'm scared to death my father'll catch us!"

"It's all right," said Alfred. "He's down below holding the ladder."

"A bride wears white! It is a symbol of goodness, of purity ..."

"How come the groom wears black?"

* * *

A Swedish couple were at city hall applying for a marriage license. "Your name?" asked the clerk.

"Ole Oleson."

"And yours?"

"Lena Oleson."

"Any connection?"

"Only vunce," she blushed. "He yumped me!"

* * *

A very attractive chorine was shopping in the department store. Approaching the salesgirl in the lingerie section, she asked, "Do you have a red-checked nightgown?"

"Red-checked?" repeated the startled clerk.

"Yes," said the chorus girl. "You see, I'm getting married and I'd like to be able to surprise my husband with *something!*"

* * *

The bride-to-be was advised by the marriage counselor never to disrobe completely in front of her husband before retiring.

One night, six weeks after the wedding, the husband said to his bride, "Is there any insanity in your family?"

"No," she said, "Why?"

"Because," he said, "I was wondering why you haven't taken off your hat since we've been married."

* * *

PAJAMAS
Items of clothing newlyweds place beside their bed in case of fire

* * *

At the bachelor dinner for the groom the night before the wedding, he was asked if he was going to be a man or a mouse.

"What's the difference?" he inquired.

"If you're a man you'll do it the first night," explained one of the fellows. "If you're a mouse you'll wait till the second night."

"I'm a rat," he said. "I did it last night!"

* * *

The bride-to-be came to the last beautifully wrapped package. Opening it, she found this note: *Wear this on your wedding night and you will be sure to wow him.*

The bride-to-be looked through all the tissue paper and smiled. The package was empty.

The newlyweds wanted to fly United but the stewardess objected.

* * *

Fay had planned to get her driver's license before the wedding so that she could share the driving on their honeymoon. As fate would have it, Fay became so absorbed with wedding details, she never got further than making an application for a beginner's permit.

On the wedding day, shortly after the couple had left the reception, the bride reappeared at the front door.

"What happened?" asked an aunt.

"Oh, nothing," said the bride, heading for the stairs. "I just forgot my learner's permit!"

* * *

Hear about the sleepy bride who couldn't keep herself awake for a second?

* * *

After a week in a small-town motel room without going out, the groom decided to take his bride to a movie. "Hey, honey," he called to her in the bathroom, "would you like to see *Oliver Twist?*"

"No thanks. I've seen it do everything else!"

SUSPICION

When your beautiful new wife has forty-six towels in her hope chest—each from a different hotel

*   *   *

Just before the wedding, the best man took the groom aside and said, "You don't want to marry this girl. Everybody in Springfield has had her."

"So," said the groom, "is Springfield such a big place?"

*   *   *

An uneducated immigrant had been thrown over by the bride for the rich young groom. The rejected suitor stood disconsolately in a corner after the ceremony at the church. "Don't take it so hard," said the best man, "there's just as good fish in the sea as ever were caught."

"Yah, sure," replied the man, "but I hate to lose fish after I have hook in, maybe sixteen, seventeen times."

*   *   *

The couple were just pronounced man and wife. As the groom kissed the bride, a child's voice piped up from the rear: "Mama, is he sprinkling the pollen on her now?"

61

Telling some brides what they should know on their wedding night is like giving a fish a bath.

* * *

As a wedding night prank, the younger sister cut the bride's nightgown in half. As the newlyweds were undressing, the husband said, "Now don't you peek!"
The bride, trying to get into her nightgown said, "Oh, it's much too short!"
"You went and peeked after all," said the groom.

* * *

Herbert and his new bride decided to spend their first night together in his parents' home. His parents decided to listen through the wall and do everything the newlyweds did.
After the couple had made love three times and were getting ready for a fourth, the boy's father banged on the wall. "Herbert stop!" he shouted. "You're killing your mother!"

* * *

CUPID'S PROPHECY
If a married couple put a coin in a box for every time they make love during the first year and take one out for every time in all the succeeding years, they will never run out of coins.

When the newlyweds realized that the parents were listening through the wall in the next room, the bride and groom decided to pack their luggage and go to a motel.

The parents continued to listen, thinking the newlyweds were still making love. The bride's hastily packed suitcase wouldn't shut. "Let me sit on it!" she said.

"No, I'll sit on it!" said the groom.

"Let's both sit on it at once!" said the bride.

The father pulled open the door and shouted, "This I gotta see!"

* * *

Darren McGavin, the energetic TV and motion picture actor and producer, has an equally developed sense of humor. This is a favorite:

An absent-minded midwest college professor forgot his umbrella in a hotel room. When he went back, he found his room had already been taken by a newlywed couple.

He was about to knock on the door when he heard a man's voice say, "Whose little lips are these?"

"Yours, dear!" said the female voice.

"And whose little hips are these?"

"Yours, dear, yours!"

"Hey," shouted the professor over the transom, "when you come to the umbrella, that's mine!"

Mike Gerber, the California lamp mogul, remembered an army buddy who had come back from overseas in the morning. He got married in the afternoon, and that night in the motel, his bride knelt beside the honeymoon bed to say her prayers.

"Now I lay me down to sleep," she began.

"That's what *you* think!" said the soldier, fluffing up his pillow.

*　　*　　*

The groom knocked at his wife's door at midnight.

"I bet I know what you're knocking for!" said the bride.

"But do you know what I'm knocking with?"

*　　*　　*

Greenberg whispered to his newly married daughter that he had put an extra wedding present of a $100 bill in one of her gloves. The bride forgot about it and was getting into the taxi to leave on her honeymoon without the gloves, when suddenly she remembered and called to her mother to run back for them.

"What is it, honey?"

"I want my gloves, Mother!"

"Gloves-shmoves," exploded Mrs. Greenberg. "Take it in your bare hand the way I did with your father!"

BRIDE'S TOAST

May you live as long as you want to,
And want to as long as you live.
If you want to and I'm asleep, wake me.
If I'm awake and don't want to, make me!

* * *

A young couple on their honeymoon had taken an upper berth on the Niagara Limited. Shortly after they climbed up, and about every two minutes thereafter, the bride exclaimed, "Oh, Arthur, I just can't convince myself that we're finally married."

This went on for an hour, until at last someone from the other end of the train shouted, "For goodness sake, Artie, will you convince her so we can all get some sleep!"

* * *

The Cockney newlyweds were retired for the night. When an hour has passed the wife said, " 'Erbert, 'ow about it?"

Herbert didn't answer. Another hour passed and she said, " 'Erbert, 'ow about it?" But still no reply.

The night passed into morning and dawn came. "Well, 'Erbert, 'ow about it?" the wife complained.

" 'Ow about what?" he asked.

" 'Ow about going to sleep?"

Stockbroker Don Burnett tells about Alan and Lorraine reaching their hotel room. The groom undressed and got into bed. The bride put on an elegant negligee and combed her hair. Then she creamed her face, manicured her nails, and put a drop of perfume behind each ear.

Alan watched this endless preparation, then hopped out of bed and started rummaging through his suitcase.

"What are you doing?" asked Lorraine.

"If this is going to be a formal affair," answered the groom, "I thought I'd better put on my spats!"

They were watching the colored lights illuminate Niagara Falls. The bride bestowed a tender kiss on the lobe of her spouse's left ear, then whispered shyly, "Did all your friends at the stag supper congratulate you?"

"Some," he admitted frankly. "But eight of them thanked me!"

* * *

The newlyweds were riding the train to Florida for their honeymoon. She fondled him under the cover of a newspaper spread on his lap. But it was a hot day and soon they fell asleep. In a little while a breeze blew away the paper.

The conductor came by. "Hey, wake up!" he said, shaking the bride gently. "Your bouquet has wilted!"

* * *

Josette Banzet Cowan, the lovely Beverly Hills charity fund-raiser, heard this one at a recent tennis tournament benefit:

The young couple had just returned from their honeymoon. All the bride's friends gathered around her and one of them asked, "How did Kevin register at the first hotel you stopped at?"

"Just fine!" replied the young bride.

The honeymooners were checking out of the hotel. "What's this item, $100 for meals?" the groom asked the clerk. "I never came down for dinner. I'm on my honeymoon."

"We're on the European plan here," replied the clerk. "It was there for you. If you didn't use it, it's not our fault!"

"Well, then, we've even," said the bridegroom. "Because you owe me $100 for making love to my wife."

"I never touched your wife!" exclaimed the clerk.

"Look, it was there for you. If you didn't use it, it's not my fault."

*   *   *

Then there was the bride who put a piece of wedding cake under her pillow for luck. Next morning, she woke up with a crumb.

*   *   *

A hillbilly boy brought back his bride to her father the morning after the wedding.

"What's the trouble?" asked her father.

"Well," said the boy, "that up-and-down motion may come natural, but that round-and-round motion had to be learned."

CUPID'S ADVICE

When you and your sweetie are in bed,
don't get scared, just go ahead.

*   *   *

On their wedding night, the bridegroom was left limping and gasping by the incredibly capable techniques used by the virgin bride.

"Where'd you learn all those tricks?" he asked.

"While you were in the army, I took a correspondence course in marriage," she explained.

"I still don't see how you could ..."

"I'll show you," she said, picking up the complimentary basket of fruit presented by the hotel. She lay down under a chair and hung an apple and an orange from it. Then she hung a banana between them. And then, while gyrating with a hip motion, she chanted: "Hit the apple, hit the orange, spin the banana, BUMP! Hit the apple, hit the ..."

*   *   *

Dennis had only been a husband a short time when he ran into Stan, the neighborhood practical joker.

"How long you married now?" asked Stan.

70

"Six weeks," declared Dennis.

"How're you getting along with your love life?" inquired Stan, wanting to put him on a little.

"Tell you the truth, not so good," moaned Dennis. "All of a sudden my wife cut me down to once a week."

"You're lucky," said Stan. "I know two guys she cut off altogether!"

* * *

The honeymoon, with its routine of making love before every meal, was over. Now came the first morning of normalcy for the newlyweds. He got up, showered, shaved, and got ready to go to his office. Then he awakened his young wife.

"It's time for breakfast, darling," he said gently.

She opened one eye, glared at him, and yawned, "Good Lord, will this never end?"

* * *

At the wedding breakfast, the groom finds that his wife has put nothing on his plate but a head of lettuce.

"What's this?" he asked.

"I just wanted to see if you eat like a rabbit, too!"

71

An Arkansas farm boy called off his wedding three days before it was supposed to take place.

"What went wrong, all of a sudden?" asked his father.

"Paw," said the boy, "I been feelin' round in Annie May's pants, and I found out she's a virgin. That's why I decided not to marry her."

"You done right, son," said the father. "If that girl ain't good enough for her own kinfolks, she ain't good enough for us neither!"

* * *

"Did you hear about Joyce? She's getting married."

"Married? I didn't even know she was pregnant!"

* * *

Lovely actress Susan Glazer tells about the new bride who asked the doctor for a sure method of birth control. "Orange juice!" responded the M.D.

"Do you take it before or after?" asked the newlywed.

"Neither," said the doctor. "Instead!"

A pretty teacher substituted for a friend who was taking a week's honeymoon. A month later, at a party, someone started to introduce the groom to her.

"Oh, I know Miss Davis very well," he said. "She substituted for my wife on our honeymoon."

* * *

The new bride was having her house painted, and when she got up one morning she noticed a spot where her husband had leaned against the door jamb.

"Would you come up here a minute?" she called downstairs to the painter. "I'd like to show you where my husband put his hand last night."

"If it's all the same to you, lady," said the painter, "could I just have a can of beer?"

* * *

A young bride consulted a doctor about a dependable way not to conceive. "I recommend an exercise," said the M.D. "You cross your legs and shake your head!"

Maury Wills, the ex-star shortstop for the Los Angeles Dodgers, and now an excellent baseball commentator on NBC, told this one to pals at the World Series:

Bernie was getting married that night, but during the afternoon he was in a car accident. After an examination the doctor informed him that he was all right except for a severe ligament laceration in a most awkward place, and it would be necessary to apply a protective covering.

The physician made a splint out of four small strips of narrow wood and some bandages. Bernie was heartbroken. Of all days for this to happen! But there was nothing he could do.

That night when he and his new bride got to the motel, she started to disrobe in striptease fashion. She revealed her shoulders and said, "Look, Bernie, never been touched by any man!"

Then stripping to the waist, she said, "Look, darling, no other man's eyes have ever gazed upon this!"

As she dropped her slip, Bernie threw open his robe. "That's nothing." he said. "Look at this! Still in the original crate!"

* * *

THE CONCEIVERS

Maybelle was afraid of needles. The doctor had tried for ten minutes to convince her that this would not be painful. "I tell you this won't hurt," he said.

"Someone once said the same thing to my sister," muttered Maybelle, "and now she can't button her coat!"

* * *

PREGNANT
Past tense of virgin

* * *

Am I a people?
No, you are a chicken.
Do chickens come from people?
No, chickens come from eggs.
Are eggs born?
No, eggs are laid.
Are people laid?
No, some people are chicken.

75

Did you hear about the beautiful Egyptian Princess who was laid in a tomb and became a mummy?

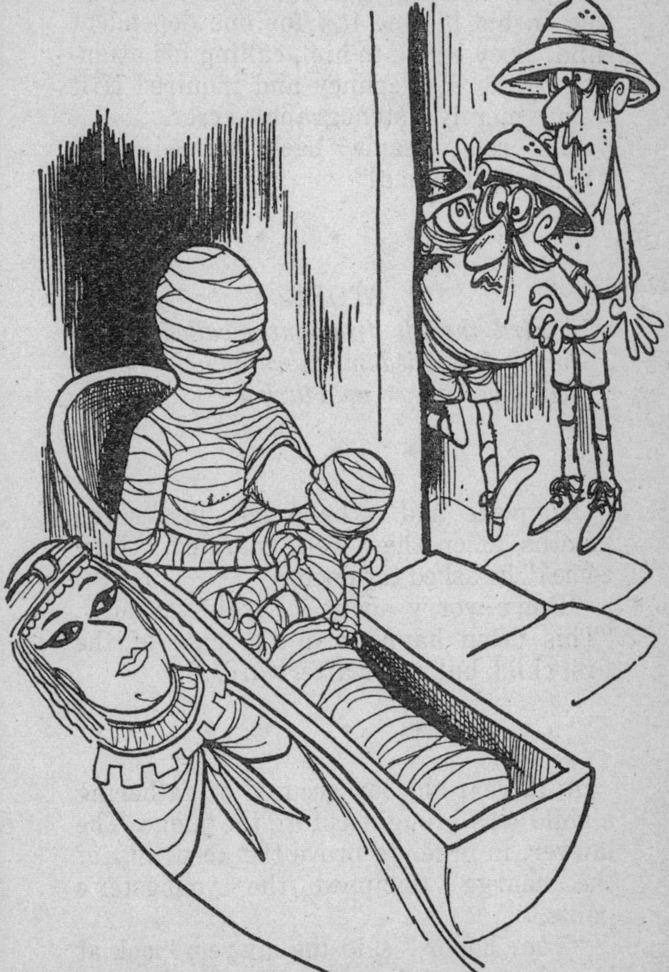

Income tax officials were at a loss to understand why a man, who claimed he was not married, also claimed an exemption in his income tax for one dependent child. They wrote to him, calling his attention to the discrepancy and inquired if it wasn't merely a stenographic error.

His reply came back immediately: "You're telling me!"

* * *

STORK
A bird that is frequently called to account for misdemeanors which should really be blamed on a lark

* * *

His wife had a baby boy just seven months after they were married. "How come?" he asked the doctor.

"Don't worry about it," said the M.D. "This often happens in the case of the first child, but never afterwards."

* * *

A 12-year-old boy accused of fathering a child was brought before the judge. The lawyer, in order to prove the absurdity of the charge, unzipped the youngster's pants.

"Your honor," said the lawyer, "look at this tiny organ, this immature equipment. How could a boy father a baby with this little, undeveloped..."

"Hey, mister," whispered the boy, "you better quit stroking me like that or we're gonna lose this case!"

*　*　*

Robert Dachman, Chicago's champion fund-raiser for Little City, tells about the son who rushed into his father's office and announced: "I got a girl in trouble, Pop, and if I don't get her out, we're all going to be in trouble!"

"How much?" asked the parent.

"Ten thousand!"

A few days later, a second son pleaded, "I need $15,000. I knocked up a girl and I've got to have it."

The next day, the daughter came home. "Papa," she confessed. "I'm pregnant!"

"Thank God! Business is picking up!"

*　*　*

Welcome, welcome little stranger
You've made two hearts very glad
You took a big load off of Mother
And made room for dear old Dad.

*　*　*

A woman passenger on an incredibly slow train traveling from New York to Chicago gave birth to a baby. "Lady," said the conductor, "you should have known better than to get on the train in that condition."

"I wasn't in that condition when I got on the train!" came the reply.

MISCARRIAGE
Love's labor lost

*   *   *

For years his friends had chided Hugh about being impotent. So it was with great glee that he reported his spouse had just come from the doctor's and announced she was pregnant.

"Well, why not?" teased a buddy. "Nobody ever doubted your wife."

*   *   *

Shapiro's daughter came home in tears. "Daddy," she whimpered, "that rich Mr. Green betrayed me and I'm going to be a mother!"

"I'll kill him!" shouted Shapiro, dashing out the door. He rushed over to the wealthy man's plush apartment and told him what he was going to do.

"Don't get excited," said Green. "I'm not running away. I intend to do right by your daughter. If she has a boy, she'll get $50,000. If it's a girl, I'll give her $35,000. Is that fair?"

"Yes," agreed Shapiro. "And if it's a miscarriage, will you give her another chance?"

*   *   *

MOTHER FROCKER
A seamstress for pregnant women

You can be knocked down, too!

A young pregnant woman asked the doctor what position she would have to lie in to give birth to the baby.

"The same position," he replied, "you were in when you started it."

"Good heavens!" she exclaimed. "Do you mean I've got to drive around Central Park in a taxi for two hours with my feet hanging out the window?"

*   *   *

A pretty blonde boarded a crowded bus and asked a man to get up and give her his seat. "I'm pregnant!" she announced.

The man got up grudgingly and said, "You don't look very filled out. How long have you been pregnant?"

"About thirty minutes, and I feel like hell!"

*   *   *

It happened in the hills of Tennessee. Martha Mae had just given birth to her twelfth child. As she was leaving the hospital with her latest in her arms, her nurse good-naturedly remarked, "I guess we'll be seeing you next year just about this same time."

"No, you won't! That's for sure," she answered confidently.

"How do you know?" the nurse asked.

"Becuz me an' m'man jest found out whut's causin' 'em."

Doctor: Go home and tell your husband.
Girl: But doctor, I'm not married.
Doctor: Well, then tell your lover.
Girl: I don't have a lover!
Doctor: All right, then go home and tell your mother to prepare for the second coming of Christ!

* * *

A boy was trying to get up the nerve to pop the question to his girl. He went to his father for advice. "Dad, what did you say to Mother when you proposed?"

"All I said was, 'The hell you say!' We were married the next day!"

* * *

HYSTERECTOMY
An operation that removes the baby carriage but leaves the playpen in good condition

* * *

Junior had reached the age of curiosity. One morning he walked in the house and asked, "Mommy, where did you meet Daddy?"

"At a picnic," she replied.

"Was I with you?"

"Not when I went, but I brought you back!"

Bill Blustein, Beverly Hills barrister to the stars, heard this one at a Bar Association convention:

A French lawyer visiting this country spoke to his American counterparts denying the allegation that French law cases were always about sex.

"Take the case I'm handling now," he said. "It's merely a family problem. My client was in love with a girl, but she was afraid of losing her virginity and made him promise he would not penetrate her maidenhead.

"He did exactly as he promised, but just at that special moment her mother burst into the bedroom, saw what was going on, became furiously angry, and gave my client a tremendous kick in the behind.

"He relieved himself, the girl got pregnant, and my client claims that the *girl's mother is the father of the child!*"

* * *

PREGNANT

A woman all swelled up over her mate's handiwork

* * *

Cliff Norton, one of television's fine character actors, tells about the movie star who returned from a year's shooting in Europe to discover that his wife had

given birth to a baby boy the week before his arrival home.

"But I don't understand how this could
have happened," he bellowed. "I've been
away on location for over twelve months!"

"Yeah," said his wife, "but your stand-
in hasn't!"

* * *

Two farmers, Clem and Clyde, met one
morning on a dusty road. "Git yer spring
plantin' done yet?" asked Clem.

"Nope!" answered Clyde.

"How come?"

"Tractor's broke."

"Who broke it?"

"Hired hand."

"Same one thet knocked up yer daughter, Emma Lou?"

"Yep."

"Clumsy varmint, ain't he?"

* * *

The pretty young lady went to her doctor for an examination. Her distress was
fairly obvious—she was *that* way again.

"Three children," said the doctor. "One
each year for the past three years, and
now a fourth on the way. Your husband
must love you very much."

"Oh, I'm not married," she said.

"Then why don't you get married?"

"Because the guy doesn't appeal to me!"

Then there was the family of hillbillies who lived near a camp for parachute jumpers. They had nine boys and eight girls.

One day about fifty paratroopers were put on maneuvers and all fifty of them bailed out over the hillbilly shack. One of the kids saw them and ran into the house shouting, "Oh, Pa! Come on outside. The stork is delivering them full-growed now!"

* * *

OPTIMIST

A pregnant girl who rubs vanishing cream on her tummy

* * *

Genial Jim Seidel, resident M.D. at California's Harbor General Hospital, related this recent experience:

On her first day out of bed the new mother put on her bathrobe and walked down the hospital corridor to the public telephone booths. She was thumbing through one of the directories when her doctor happened by. "And what are you doing out here?" he asked.

"I'm looking through the phone book to find a nice name for my baby," she said.

"You don't have to do that. The hospital supplies a little booklet to all new

mothers listing every first name you could possibly think of."

"You don't understand," she explained. "The baby already has a *first* name."

* * *

Two babies, in adjacent cribs at the hospital, were gurgling at each other one fine day. If any of the nurses had been able to translate their baby sounds, this is the conversation they would have overheard:

Baby 1: I was born last Tuesday. What about you?

Baby 2: I came in Thursday. By the way, what time do we eat?

Baby 1: In about fifteen minutes. I can hardly wait for that bottle.

Baby 2: You mean you're on a bottle already? I'm still on the breast.

Baby 1: I used to be, but they took me off.

Baby 2: Hey, you've had both. Which do you like better—breast-feeding or bottle-feeding?

Baby 1: Bottle feeding. That way you don't get so many cigarette ashes in your eyes.

* * *

QUADRUPLETS
That's when one goes into one, one time, and there's four to carry.

Andy Thomas, the talented pianist-conductor for many of America's top singing stars, warms up musicians at rehearsal with this one:

A distinguished-looking old soul of 85 summers consulted his doctor. "I'm 85 years old," he said, "and my wife just gave birth to a baby. Do you think I could do it again?"

"Tell me," asked the M.D. "Do you think you did it the first time?"

Three babies were being pushed through the supermarket while their mothers shopped. One remarked, "Look at that! She's buying Pablum, and I *hate* the stuff."

"Mine's buying spinach," said another. "That's the worst."

"You don't have anything to complain about," said the third baby. "How'd you like to be awakened at three in the morning by having a cold, wet tit stuck in your mouth that tasted like a White Owl cigar."

* * *

Harris, aged 90, walked into the doctor's office and asked for a blood test. "A blood test?" exclaimed the physician. "You mean at your age you still want to get married?"

"Tell you the truth," said the old man, "I don't really *want* to—I've *got* to!"

* * *

MOTHER'S DAY
Nine months after Father's Day

* * *

When Grace met her friend Marge on the street one afternoon, she noticed that Marge was well along in her pregnancy.

"I'd give anything to have a baby," said Grace, "but I guess it's hopeless!"

"My husband felt that way, too," said Marge, "but as you can see I'm eight months pregnant."

"What did you do?"

"Went to a faith healer."

"Oh, we tried that," said Grace. "My husband and I went there for six months."

"Don't be silly," said Marge. "Go alone!"

*　　*　　*

Horowitz had three daughters whom he wanted to marry off. It was the custom in his country to offer a dowry with an eligible child. A prospective suitor stood before the father. "With this one," said Horowitz, "I'll give $1,000. She's a little knock-kneed."

The young man turned her down.

"All right, with this one," said Horowitz, "I'll give $2,000. She's a little cross-eyed!"

The boy shook his head emphatically.

"Okay," said the father, "with the third one, I'll give $10,000."

"Why? She's so beautiful?"

"Well," said Horowitz, "she's a little pregnant!"

*　　*　　*

SHIFTLESS BASTARD
Baby conceived in car with automatic transmission

"I'm going to have a little one,"
Said the girl, so gay and frisky.
When her boyfriend up and fainted,
She told him she meant whiskey.

* * *

Mrs. Giordano had come from Italy only a short time before. She and her husband were happy except for one thing. So far they hadn't received a little bundle from heaven. Mr. Giordano persuaded his wife to see a physician.

Reluctantly, Mrs. Giordano went to an obstetrician. After the examination, the doctor said, "I'm sorry to have to tell you but you have a deficiency in passion. If you ever have a baby it will be a miracle."

That night, she explained the doctor's diagnosis to her husband. "The doctor he's-a say I'm-a got a fish in da passage, and if I'm-a ever have a bambino she's-a gonna be a mackerel."

* * *

Fifty-three-year-old Flanagan was overjoyed to learn that his wife had given birth to triplets and in his enthusiasm attempted to barge into the delivery room to see her. The nurse stopped him and said, "You can't go in there, you're not sterile!"

"That, lady, is quite obvious!" said Flanagan proudly.

Sandra Giles, the talented tennis-playing actress, told this one at a recent Bobby Riggs affair:

Johnny, aged seven, was in love with Susan, aged six, the girl next door. He confided to his father that they planned to get married.

"What are you going to do about money?" asked his father with pretended gravity.

"I have my allowance," replied the little boy, "and Susie has nearly $1.20 in her piggy bank."

"That's fine for now," said Johnny's father, "but what will you do when the children come?"

"We decided that if Susie lays any eggs, we're going to step on them!"

*   *   *

PERAMBULATOR
Last year's fun on wheels

Johnny Gilbert, the handsome television emcee, overheard a woman talking to her six-year-old son Tommy in a supermarket:

"If you don't stop biting your fingernails you'll get a big stomach like that lady," warned his mother, pointing to a pregnant woman.

Tommy stared at the woman, and as they passed he whispered to her, "Lady, I know what you've been doing!"

Dick had just finished making love to his newest conquest and was getting dressed. He kissed the girl passionately and then said, "Suppose, my dear, you were to find yourself, er, ah, you know, suppose something went wrong, what would you do?"

"Why, why, I'd kill myself!"

"That's my girl," said Dick, patting her on the shoulder.

* * *

UNBORN IDIOT
A little inside dope

* * *

Advertising exec Judy Campbell-Broom brought this one over with her from England:

Food had been scarce in Great Britain. Then all of a sudden a shipment of fresh eggs arrived from the United States. One store received its allotment and the proprietor immediately put up a sign in the window:

THESE EGGS ARE FOR
EXPECTANT MOTHERS ONLY

A line formed in front of the store and one woman whispered to the clerk, "I'd consider it a big favor if you'd put a dozen eggs under the counter for me. I'll call for them in the morning."

A clever New York dress designer is doing a skyrocketing business. He's developed a line of teen-age maternity fashions in their school colors.

*　*　*

"Will my husband be permitted to stay with me during the delivery?" asked the patient of her obstetrician in the Maternity Ward.

"Oh, yes," replied the doctor. "I believe the father of the child should also be present at its birth."

"I don't think that'd be a good idea," said the woman. "He and my husband don't get along too well together."

*　*　*

CONTRACEPTIVE
An article to be worn on every conceivable occasion.

*　*　*

Three bachelors were kidding Lou, the married man among them. "You've been hitched five years now, Lou, how come you have no children?" asked one of them. Then trying to make a bad pun he added, "Is your wife *unbearable?*"

"Or," said another guy, "is she *inconceivable?*"

"Maybe she's *impregnable*," joked the third man.

"No, boys, you're all wrong," lamented Lou. "My wife is *insurmountable* and *inscrutable!*"

*   *   *

Rudy DiLuca, one of Carol Burnett's clever comedy writers, contributed this cutie:

The first male and female astronauts land on Mars and discover there is life. A group of Martians show the astronauts all the advanced techniques on the planet as well as a plant where babies are made.

"A piece of dough is shaped like a little girl or boy, placed on a conveyor belt, and sent through an incubator," explained the Martian leader. "Ten minutes later, out comes an infant."

"We make babies differently on earth," said the female astronaut.

"Please show us!" requested a Martian.

The astronauts removed their clothes and had intercourse right before the Martians. When they'd finished, the Martian leader asked, "Where's the baby?"

"That comes in nine months," explained the girl.

"If it takes nine months," asked the leader, "why were you in such a hurry there at the end?"

*   *   *